*The Campus History Series*

# GEORGIA TECH

*The Campus History Series*

# GEORGIA TECH

MATTHEW HILD AND DAVID L. MORTON

ARCADIA
PUBLISHING

Copyright © 2018 by Matthew Hild and David L. Morton
ISBN 978-1-4671-2960-2

Published by Arcadia Publishing
Charleston, South Carolina

Printed in the United States of America

Library of Congress Control Number: 2018941675

For all general information, please contact Arcadia Publishing:
Telephone 843-853-2070
Fax 843-853-0044
E-mail sales@arcadiapublishing.com
For customer service and orders:
Toll-Free 1-888-313-2665

Visit us on the Internet at www.arcadiapublishing.com

*This book is dedicated to George P. Burdell in recognition of his legendary contributions to Georgia Tech.*

# CONTENTS

# ACKNOWLEDGMENTS

We would like to thank the following members of the Georgia Tech community for their assistance or support: Aimee Anderson, G. Wayne Clough, Mike Flynn, August W. Giebelhaus, Kirk Henderson, Rebecca Keane, Robert C. McMath, Karen Milchus, Christopher Moore, Mac Pitts, Jacqueline Jones Royster, Eric Schatzberg, Marilyn Somers, and Jody Thompson. We would also like to extend our thanks to the Georgia Tech Athletic Association, the Ivan Allen College of Liberal Arts, the School of History and Sociology, and especially the Georgia Tech Archives.

We are also grateful to Stacia Bannerman, Jonny Foster, and Sarah Ybarra at Arcadia Publishing for their helpfulness.

All photographs appear courtesy of the Georgia Tech Archives except as noted.

# INTRODUCTION

The creation of Georgia Tech in the 1880s reflected two significant trends, one of which was national and the other distinctly Southern. At the national level, the establishment of colleges and universities devoted to instruction in engineering started becoming more common; notable examples include the Massachusetts Institute of Technology in 1861, the Worcester Polytechnic Institute (also located in Massachusetts) in 1865, the Stevens Institute of Technology in New Jersey in 1871, and the Virginia Polytechnic Institute and State University in 1872. That this trend began earlier in the North than in the South is not surprising, since the former region was already more industrialized than the latter before the Civil War, which in turn left the South even more bereft of manufacturing and in economic ruin. By the 1880s, a group of men that included Georgians such as journalist Henry W. Grady of Atlanta and textile industrialist John Fletcher Hanson of Macon were promoting a "New South creed" that emphasized industrialization as the path to the South's economic recovery. While Grady focused his efforts on attracting much-needed capital from Northern and foreign investors to Atlanta, Hanson used the *Macon Telegraph and Messenger*, which he owned, to launch a campaign in 1882 to create a technical institution of higher education in the state. He found an ally in Macon attorney Nathaniel E. Harris, who won election to the state legislature later that year with Hanson's support. Shortly after taking office, Harris introduced a bill to appoint a committee to examine the possibility of creating a school of technology as a branch of the University of Georgia.

That committee held its first meeting in May 1883 in Atlanta. Its efforts reached fruition on October 13, 1885, when Gov. Henry D. McDaniel signed a bill that created a technological school with an appropriation of $65,000 and the stipulation that it be, nominally at least, a branch of the University of Georgia, although the technical institute would have its own board of trustees. Harris would serve as the chairman of the Georgia Tech board of trustees until his death in 1929. (He also served as the governor of Georgia from 1915 until 1917.) The bill did not specify where the technical institute would be located. Athens, Atlanta, Macon, Milledgeville, and Penfield all made bids. The selection of Atlanta, which greatly disappointed Hanson and Harris, occurred in part due to the influence of Grady and the *Atlanta Constitution*, which he edited.

The Georgia School of Technology—its original name—opened on Friday, October 5, 1888, and for the first of countless times, a steam whistle sounded on the campus that day. Isaac S. Hopkins stepped into the role of president of the new school, having left the vice presidency at Emory University to take the position. Eighty-five students, all white males, constituted the initial student body, and they would divide their 10-hour school days between the Shop Building and the Academic Building (now informally known as the Tech Tower). The school did not grow rapidly in terms of either facilities or enrollment. In 1896, a new president, Lyman Hall, replaced Hopkins, and Georgia Tech added two new majors, electrical engineering and civil engineering; until then, mechanical engineering had been the sole degree program. During Hall's tenure, the school added two more majors, textile engineering in 1899 and engineering chemistry in 1901.

Despite financially lean times during the first two decades of the 20th century, Georgia Tech made steady progress in terms of enrollment, curriculum, facilities, and visibility. Enrollment grew to 511 for the 1904–1905 academic year. On October 20, 1905, Pres. Theodore Roosevelt made a visit to campus, speaking to some 500 students from the steps of the Tech Tower and then shaking hands with each of them. In 1906, Andrew Carnegie donated $20,000 for the construction of a library building on campus, which opened the following year. Located next to the Tech Tower, that building is still in use as the Carnegie Building, which houses the office of the president. Georgia Tech athletics also received a great boost in this era with the arrival of John Heisman, already a successful college football coach, in 1904. Thirteen years later, he led Tech to its first national football championship. By then, the United States was involved in World War I, and consequently, a unit of the Reserve Officers Training Corps (ROTC) was established at Tech in March 1918. ROTC is still active on campus a century later.

In 1922, Marion L. Brittain assumed the presidency of Georgia Tech, and he went on to hold that position for 22 years, longer than any of his predecessors or, so far, successors. According to the institute's centennial history, *Engineering the New South: Georgia Tech, 1885–1985*, Brittain's leadership "resulted in an outburst of building activity, curriculum additions, faculty improvements, and finally a reorganization of the University System of Georgia." Effective on New Year's Day 1932, the newly established Board of Regents of the University System of Georgia assumed the oversight and direction of the state's public institutions of higher learning. Brittain also played a major role in Georgia Tech receiving a $300,000 grant from the Daniel Guggenheim Fund for the Promotion of Aeronautics in March 1930, which was quite a coup for a public college, especially since the Great Depression had begun just over four months earlier. With this grant, Georgia Tech established the Daniel Guggenheim School of Aeronautics (now the Daniel Guggenheim School of Aerospace Engineering). Another significant development of this era occurred in 1934, when the board of regents and the state legislature approved the creation of the State Engineering Experiment Station at Tech. Fifty years later, this became the Georgia Tech Research Institute (GTRI), still an integral part of the institute today. Nevertheless, a shortage of funds and declining enrollments plagued Georgia Tech during the darkest years of the Great Depression.

Brittain confronted an even greater crisis after the Depression, however, when Gov. Eugene Talmadge's efforts to subvert the autonomy of the board of regents led the Southern Association of Colleges and Secondary Schools to suspend the accreditation of all 10 of Georgia's white public colleges and universities as of September 1, 1942. Subsequently, Brittain, along with many Tech faculty and students (many of whom were under the voting age of, at that time, 21) and their counterparts at other colleges in the state, worked for the defeat of Talmadge, who lost the Democratic primary and governorship to Ellis Arnall in the 1942 elections. Under Arnall's leadership, accreditation was quickly restored to the 10 colleges and universities. The independence and autonomy of the board of regents would subsequently be protected in the Georgia Constitution.

World War II proved to be a turning point in the history of Georgia Tech. The most immediate result of American entry into the war following the Japanese attack on Pearl Harbor on December 7, 1941, was that many students left campus for military service, either voluntarily or after being drafted. Many faculty members, too, left campus, either going into the service themselves or entering into government positions that called for expertise in certain areas of engineering. On the other hand, many other young men came to the campus, as Georgia Tech became a site for both the V-12 Navy College Training Program and the Army Specialized Training Program. Even more significantly than any of these developments, however, the war soon exerted a major impact on research at Georgia Tech, with federal government and industrial contracts accounting for more than half of its research budget for the first time in 1943. In July 1944, Blake Van Leer, a US Army colonel, became the fifth president of Georgia Tech. He was also the first bona fide engineer to become the president of the institute, having earned a degree in electrical engineering from Purdue University in 1915.

From this point on, Georgia Tech became more of a research institution, a development that was reflected in its name being changed from the Georgia School of Technology to the Georgia Institute of Technology in 1948. Thanks in no small part to the GI Bill of 1944, which provided veterans with funds for enrolling in college, enrollment at Tech rose from about 2,000 in 1944 to 5,000 four years later. The size of the faculty expanded similarly, from 125 to over 400 during that period. In July 1946, George C. Griffin (civil engineering, class of 1922), one of the most legendary figures in the history of Georgia Tech, began his 18-year tenure as dean of students.

World War II also led to the possibility of coeducation, or the admission of female students, at Georgia Tech being considered; other American engineering schools were admitting women during the war. A column in the *Technique* in 1947 bluntly opined, "Coeds at Tech? Never!" Actually, women had been allowed to matriculate at Georgia Tech's Evening School of Commerce starting in 1917. This downtown branch of Georgia Tech opened in 1913, and in 1933, the board of regents turned it into a unit of the University of Georgia. Eventually, it became Georgia State University. But while females had been allowed to earn degrees from Tech's Evening School of Commerce, they could not do so on the North Avenue campus. Van Leer, however, proved to be a cautious but committed advocate of the right of qualified female high school graduates to earn an engineering or architecture degree at Tech. So, too, did head librarian Dorothy Crosland and the president's wife, Ella Van Leer, who quietly encouraged the Woman's Chamber of Commerce of Atlanta to press the matter in early 1952. On April 9 of that year, the board of regents voted seven to five to allow female students to enter Georgia Tech. Two women, Elizabeth Herndon of Atlanta—a mother and World War II widow—and Barbara Diane Michel of Houston, enrolled at Tech in the fall quarter of 1952.

By then, a series of cases involving segregated schools was making its way through the federal courts, where it would eventually coalesce in the US Supreme Court decision of *Brown v. Board of Education of Topeka, Kansas*, in May 1954, which mandated an end to segregation in public educational institutions. The integration of grade schools as well as institutions of higher learning in the South would prove to be a difficult process, fraught with additional lawsuits, court rulings, and infamous riots. In Georgia, the case of *Holmes v. Danner* led to the admission of two African American students into the University of Georgia in January 1961. A small riot broke out on that campus shortly after the two students were admitted, and Georgia Tech president Edwin D. Harrison began taking steps, including an open meeting with students, to ensure that Georgia Tech would be able to integrate peacefully and without any embarrassing incidents. Associate dean of students James E. Dull also worked to ensure as smooth an integration process as possible. Three African American male students entered Georgia Tech in the fall quarter of 1961. G. Wayne Clough (civil engineering, class of 1964; master of science, civil engineering, class of 1965), a student at that time and later the first alumnus to serve as the president of Georgia Tech, recalls Dean Griffin warning students that any troublemakers would be expelled, and no such trouble ever occurred. In 1965, Ronald Yancey earned a degree in electrical engineering and became the first African American to graduate from Georgia Tech. Three years later, the Department of Social Sciences hired the institute's first African American instructor, William Peace. In 2010, the institutional descendant of the Department of Social Sciences, the Ivan Allen College of Liberal Arts, appointed the first African American dean in the history of Georgia Tech, Jacqueline Jones Royster.

During the late 20th century, Georgia Tech would make the leap from being one of the top technological schools in the Southeast to being one of the best in the nation and the world. The increased national emphasis on STEM education (science, technology, engineering, and mathematics) during the Cold War played a significant role in Tech's progress. In 1963, the institute dedicated the $4.5-million Neely Nuclear Research Center one year after creating a nuclear engineering department. The appointment of Joseph M. Pettit as the president of Georgia Tech in 1972 further facilitated the growing focus on research; when Pettit's tenure ended upon his death in 1986, the *New York Times* stated that it was he "who was credited with making the Georgia Institute of Technology a top-flight research institution." Pettit had left Stanford University, where he was the dean of engineering, to lead Georgia Tech, and he also served as the president of the American Society for Engineering Education. Pettit oversaw a booming era for Georgia Tech in which the value of research contracts and grants that it received increased more than eightfold.

Pettit's successor, John Patrick "Pat" Crecine, served as the ninth president of Georgia Tech from 1987 until 1994. Crecine proved to be a controversial figure, but he oversaw and helped institute substantial changes that enhanced Tech's profile and reputation while also broadening its degree programs. The creation of what was originally called the Ivan Allen College of Management, Policy, and International Affairs in 1990 led to the establishment of Tech's first doctoral program in the humanities (history of technology) in 1992, an important step in the institute's transition to a full-fledged university. Crecine also oversaw the creation of the College of Computing and the College of Sciences. In 1990, Georgia Tech opened its first international campus (Georgia Tech–Lorraine) in Metz, France.

In 1996, Atlanta hosted the Olympics, the result of a campaign by city leaders in which Crecine played a major role. Georgia Tech served as the site of the Olympic Village and many of the athletic events. The considerable amount of construction that occurred in preparation transformed the campus significantly, as was chronicled in the 1996 edition of the *Blueprint*. (One of the new structures, the Kessler Campanile, was subsequently incorporated into the Georgia Tech logo that is still in use today.) Crecine, however, had resigned by the time the Olympics arrived. His successor, G. Wayne Clough, led Georgia Tech from 1994 until 2008, when he left to become the secretary of the Smithsonian Institution. During Clough's tenure, Georgia Tech rose into the top 10 in national rankings of public universities. Clough also presided over the construction of Technology Square, which opened in 2003 and helped revitalize what had been a somewhat blighted part of Atlanta's Midtown neighborhood. In 2010, Clough was named president emeritus, and he returned to the campus with an office after retiring from the Smithsonian in 2014.

G.P. "Bud" Peterson became the 11th president of Georgia Tech in 2009. During his tenure, Georgia Tech has continued to climb in the national rankings, and the student body, which now numbers more than 29,000 undergraduate and graduate students, has become more diverse and more impressive in its academic credentials than at any point in the institute's history. The annual economic contribution of Georgia Tech to the state economy is now approximately $3 billion. Surely this represents the fulfillment of the vision of John Fletcher Hanson and the state's other New South boosters who argued in the early to mid-1880s that a technological institution of higher learning would benefit the state's economy. Even those men probably could not have imagined, however, the degree of impact in so many significant ways beyond mere economic measurements that would ultimately emanate from what started as a small campus on North Avenue in 1888.

# *One*

# THE CAMPUS

The Georgia School of Technology was established before lawmakers and advocates had even settled on a general location for the campus. The committee formed in 1886 considered several places, including Athens and Macon, before settling on Atlanta. Then came the process of picking one of several proposed plots of land. Finally, by early 1887, the committee settled on a tract north of Atlanta known as Peters Park on North Avenue, with Cherry Street as the western border. The owner, Richard Peters, agreed to donate four acres initially and make additional land available at $2,000 per acre. Even then, the campus was surrounded on all sides by land, some of it already developed, divided into multiple parcels with several different owners. The piecemeal growth of the campus through the purchase of increasingly expensive urban land continues to this day. By about 1900, the campus was still just about 10 acres, though Pres. Kenneth G. Matheson led the effort to expand it to about 25 acres between 1906 and 1923. Much of the land available to the school was north of campus, while areas on the other three sides were, for various reasons, nearly unattainable. Tech's prize money from winning the Rose Bowl in 1928 went to the purchase of 10 acres north of campus between Fifth and Eighth Streets. The land, Rose Bowl Field, remained relatively undeveloped for many years and was used for athletics, ROTC drills, and other activities. Presidents Harrison and Van Leer aggressively pursued land purchases, with Harrison adding 128 acres and Van Leer another 51. Since World War II, Tech presidents have benefitted from patience, timing, and sometimes government resources aimed at urban renewal to make strategic purchases of some of the more blighted areas adjacent to campus. The most recent expansion took place under Pres. G. Wayne Clough, creating Technology Square at Fifth and Spring Streets, east of campus and on the other side of Interstate 75/85, which had long been Tech's eastern boundary.

Georgia Tech's original campus consisted of the Shop Building, on the left, and the Academic Building, on the right. Both were visible from Peachtree Street and from nearby railroad lines. The Shop Building burned in 1892 and was rebuilt in a different form. That building was torn down in 1968. The Academic Building (Tech Tower), now known as the Lettie Pate Whitehead Evans Administration Building, houses administrative offices, including the registrar.

State congressman Clarence Knowles introduced a bill to authorize the building of Tech's first permanent dormitory in 1896. The building, completed the next year, charged $10 per month for a two-man room (sometimes three were squeezed in). Future president James E. "Jimmy" Carter lived here during his brief time studying at Tech in 1942–1943.

The Aaron French Textile Building (completed in 1898) was named after a donor, Aaron French of Pittsburgh. Institute president Lyman Hall launched a new textile program as the opening salvo in an economic war against New England, the seat of the textile equipment industry at the time.

Like many Tech buildings, Swann Dormitory, completed in 1901, was named after a benefactor who helped pay for its construction. In this case it was Janie Austell Swann, the wife of James Swann, a New York banker who became a friend of Georgia Tech after being invited to visit the campus by prominent Atlanta businessman and cotton merchant Samuel Inman.

Tech president Lyman Hall raised the funds to build the Electrical Building (later called the Electrical Engineering Building, now the Savant Building) on Cherry Street, which was dedicated in 1901. Electrical engineering was still a new field at that time, and the building helped Tech transition from a trade school to a modern college. Domenico Savant, now the building's namesake, was an electrical engineering professor and later a dean.

The chemistry laboratory opened in 1905. It was named after Lyman Hall, the Georgia Tech president who raised most of the money for its construction. The building, in the foreground, is next to the Aaron French Building, and both are used today for offices. Freshman chemistry labs were conducted at Lyman Hall until 1990.

Pres. K.G. Matheson persuaded the Andrew Carnegie Foundation to fund the construction of Tech's first library building in 1906. Carnegie libraries like this one were built in nearly 1,700 locations around the country from the late 19th to the early 20th century at colleges and in cities. This small building served as the university library from 1907 to 1953. Today, it is used for administrative offices, including the office of the president.

What is now known as the Chapin Building, completed in 1911, was originally the Joseph Brown Whitehead Memorial Hospital. Whitehead (1864–1906) had no particular connection to Georgia Tech, but his wife got involved in the fundraising effort for the building and ultimately provided a third of the funding. This was the first of three student medical facilities named after Joseph Whitehead; the second was built in 1953 and the current one in 2003.

15

The mechanical engineering building is dedicated to John Saylor Coon, the head of the mechanical engineering department and one of the building's codesigners. Its construction was authorized by the state legislature in 1910 and partly funded by the state. The building faces Cherry Street and sits at the corner of Kimball Street (now Ferst Drive). It once included a machine shop, woodshop, foundry, blacksmith shop, and classrooms.

The Carnegie Physics Building was completed in 1923 with major support from the Andrew Carnegie Foundation. It originally housed not only the physics department but also civil engineering and architecture, both of which moved from the older Mechanical Engineering Building. Situated at the corner of Bobby Dodd Way and Cherry Street, it is now called the D.M. Smith Building after beloved mathematics professor David M. Smith (1884–1962).

The old gymnasium and auditorium building was built between 1936 and 1939 using federal funding. It was the first building on campus built using reinforced concrete (previous buildings were traditional stone, masonry, and/or wood). Located at the corner of Third Street (now Bobby Dodd Way) and Techwood Drive, it enclosed the U-shaped stadium at Grant Field. The design of the building was based on the Folger Shakespeare Library in Washington, DC.

N.E. Harris Dormitory, the second dorm built in the mid-1920s at Tech, was designed by architecture professors Harold Bush-Brown, Kenneth K. Stowell, and J. Herbert Gailey. Dedicated in 1926, it was named after Nathaniel E. Harris, a politician who sponsored the bill that established Georgia Tech in 1885.

The Ceramics Building was completed in 1924 at the northwest corner of Fowler and Third Streets. A major addition was completed in 1939, funded by the federal government. For some years after ceramics moved to the Bunger Henry Building, the Navy ROTC program had its headquarters here. It is now called the Stephen Hall Building and is used by the Ivan Allen College. There was a second ROTC structure, the Military Headquarters Building, located across the street that was demolished in 2010.

When the Daniel and Florence Guggenheim Foundation in New York sponsored the creation of six new schools of aeronautics beginning in the 1920s, Georgia Tech was one of the recipients. Tech was awarded $300,000 for the construction of the new building, completed in 1931, at Cherry Street and North Avenue. At the time, Tech had the only Air Corps ROTC in the region, and had served as a ground school for aviators in World War I.

The estate of Josiah and Josephine Cloudman funded the Cloudman Dormitory for co-op students in early 1930. Like its neighbor, Harris Dormitory, it was designed by architecture professors Harold Bush-Brown and James H. Gailey through the firm they ran in Atlanta. The words "Labor and Study" adorn the vestibule, reflecting the fact that the dorm was originally intended to house students in the cooperative program.

The area south of campus on Techwood Drive was a shantytown in the early 1930s, when Tech convinced the federal government to construct a dorm there. McDaniel Dormitory (known as Techwood) opened in 1935 but was torn down in the 1990s as part of the general cleanup of the area in preparation for the Olympic Games. The dorm and other Techwood buildings were designed by Flippen Burge (architecture, class of 1916) and Preston S. Stevens (architecture, class of 1919).

Civil engineering came late to Tech, since the subject was already offered at the University of Georgia. By the 1920s, however, the civil engineering department was established and housed in the Physics Building (now D.M. Smith). The first dedicated Civil Engineering Building was completed in the late 1930s.

Work began on the Howell and Harrison Dormitories on Williams Street late in 1938. Howell was designed by architecture professor M.L. Jorgensen. Artist and Tech graduate Julian Harris (architecture, class of 1928) contributed a sculpture depicting Don Quixote that adorns the front of the building. George W. Harrison (1884–1936) was an Atlanta businessman, while Clark Howell (1863–1936) was a prominent journalist in Atlanta and later a politician.

The Engineering Research Building of 1939 provided the first substantial facilities for conducting research. In the 1940s, it was expanded and renamed after Thomas P. Hinman, a local dentist who had left Tech a gift in his will. The front of the already-expanded building was eventually hidden from view by the construction of the Rich Computing Building.

The Burge Apartments are pictured under construction on North Avenue in 1946. Because of the rapid growth in the student body after World War II and the fact that many incoming students were married, Tech built Burge as married student housing. The name honored the architecture professor Flippen Burge (see page 19), whose firm designed the building but who died shortly before it opened.

The Callaway Apartment complex was built in the late 1940s on Tenth Street and designed by architecture professors Bush-Brown, Gailey, and Heffernan. It originally housed veterans and faculty. The complex (along with numerous other campus structures) was named after Tech alumnus and benefactor Fuller E. Callaway Jr. (textile engineering, class of 1926).

Glenn, Smith, and Towers Dormitories on Campus Drive (as that part of Techwood Drive was once known) were all finished in 1947 at a cost of $1.6 million. Each was named after a donor: William Glenn (mechanical engineering, class of 1891) was the first student to register at Tech; John M. Smith was an Irish immigrant, a carriage builder by trade, and early donor to Tech; and Donigan Dean Towers (textile engineering, class of 1902) was a prominent Georgia businessman.

Few of the major buildings ever constructed on campus have been torn down, but one of them was the Harrison Hightower Textile Engineering Building. Hightower featured a classroom section and a textile manufacturing wing. It was the first fully air-conditioned building on campus, not for the sake of comfort but because of the need to control the environment for the manufacturing operations. This image shows the building under construction in 1948.

While the original President's House was on North Avenue near the current Alumni Association Building, an anonymous donor funded the construction of a new house in 1948. Designed in part by President Van Leer's wife, the resulting structure "failed to perform" its basic functions of serving as a reflection of the region and a space for entertaining guests, according to architectural historian Warren Drury. Nevertheless, it has been home to every president since.

This aerial photograph of the campus, taken around 1949, shows the limited development of the campus to the north and west. Also notable are the gymnasium and auditorium buildings at the north end of Grant Field, now removed, and Peters Park back when it did not include a parking deck.

After moving from building to building for several decades, Tech's architecture department got its own home in 1952. The building, designed by architecture department professor Paul Heffernan, was completed in 1952 with a major addition in 1980.

The S. Price Gilbert Library replaced the old Carnegie library in 1953. Designed by Professor Heffernan of the architecture department, it was named after a lawmaker, judge, and member of the board of regents who had died in 1950 and had contributed to funding the library's construction. In 1968, the library saw the addition of the Graduate Wing, today known as Dorothy M. Crosland Tower after Tech's longtime head of the library.

The low, flat-topped structure known as Skiles was originally called simply the Classroom Building when it was constructed in 1959, but it was renamed in 1964 after William Vernon Skiles, a mathematics professor who rose to executive dean before retiring in 1945.

Tech completed a major dormitory building project in 1961. Four buildings were constructed off Campus Drive (now called Techwood) near the Third Street tunnel, all named after prominent institute figures: Isaac Hopkins (first president of Georgia Tech), John Hanson (industrialist and a founder of Georgia Tech), Floyd Field (longtime dean of men) William Perry (former English professor) and Kenneth Matheson (former president).

The Electrical Engineering Department moved its headquarters to a new building at the corner of Atlantic Drive and Fourth Street in 1962. The $3.3-million building was subsequently renamed after former president Van Leer. The new building was air-conditioned, unlike the old electrical engineering building on Cherry Street, and had a distinctive circular auditorium at the south end.

The Neely Nuclear Research Center, first envisioned in 1956, was the first university-based reactor in the South. It was commissioned in 1964 and was Tech's most expensive project to date at a cost of $4.5 million. However, in the 1990s, after Tech had been selected to host the 1996 Olympics, it was seen as a security risk. Starting in 1995, the reactor was removed at a cost of about $8 million.

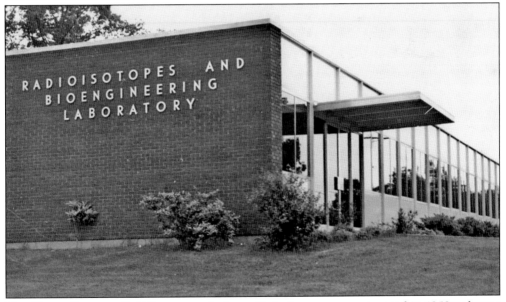

The Cherry Emerson Building, named after a Tech dean, was constructed in 1959 to house the biology department. It was originally associated with the Radioisotopes Research Center, a project that piggybacked on the construction of the Neely Nuclear Reactor.

Tech built a new home for chemical and ceramic engineering on the north side of campus in 1964. It was originally named the Bunger Building after chemical engineering professor Harold Bunger, who had risen to department head and later led the Engineering Experiment Station (now GTRI). It was renamed the Bunger-Henry Building after Arthur V. Henry, the first head of the ceramic engineering department in the early 1920s.

Bleak and nearly windowless, the Howey Physics Building was constructed in 1967 on Atlantic Drive near Ferst Drive. Joseph H. Howey was head of the physics program from the 1930s to the 1960s.

The Weber Space Sciences and Technology Building on Ferst Drive was originally named for NASA rather than Weber (and was at the corner of Hemphill Avenue and Uncle Heinie Way before the streets were reconfigured and renamed). Paul Weber was a chemical engineering professor in the 1920s and 1930s who eventually became a Tech vice president and later interim president in the 1950s. Tech broke ground on the Weber Building in 1967.

The Jesse H. Mason Building is the second home of civil engineering. The land for Mason on Hemphill Avenue was heavily developed with homes and businesses, including a nearby restaurant owned by Gov. Lester Maddox. Historians credit President Harrison with quelling widespread resistance to the demolition of the neighborhood. The Mason Building was complete by 1969.

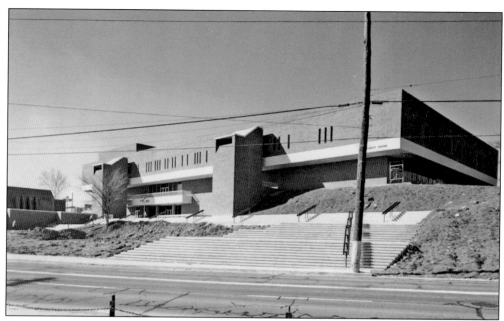

Wenn Student Center is shown here under construction around 1969. The building opened in 1970 and was rededicated in 1976 to honor industrial management professor Fred B. Wenn, who helped raise money to construct the building. The building replaced the YMCA on North Avenue (now the Alumni Association Building) as the focus of student activities. Initially, Hemphill Avenue ran in front of the building and separated the center from the rest of campus.

The Rich Electronic Computing Building replaced a special-purpose structure, the Research Annex Building, that housed Tech's first (analog) computer, the AC Network Calculator. An expansion in 1956 blocked the front of the Hinman Research Building, which was expanded at the same time, essentially joining the two. The Rich Building was expanded a third time some years later.

Dormitory building since about 1960 has been on the west side of campus. In 1969, several dorms were constructed in the area, including Fulmer, the institute's first women's dorm. Other dorms in the area include Harold E. Montag, Freeman, Hefner, and Fitten (1972), Woodruff (1984), Nelson-Shell (1992), Center Street (1995), and Eighth Street (1995). Crecine Apartments, shown here, was constructed in 1995 on West Campus near the existing Couch Building. (Courtesy of the Georgia Institute of Technology.)

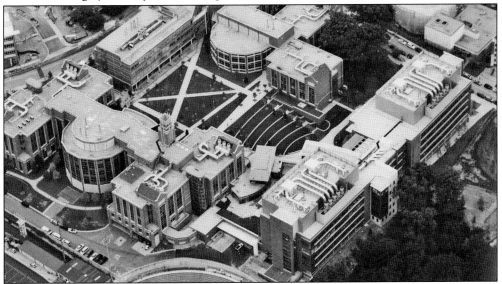

The Parker H. Petit Biotechnology Building opened in 1999 on Ferst Drive. It represented the culmination of a decades-long effort to build bioengineering and biotechnology capabilities at Tech in conjunction with Emory University. That area around Ferst Drive has become the focus of a complex of biotechnology and bioengineering facilities, including the Ford Environmental Science and Technology Building (2003), the U.A. Whitaker Building (2003), and the Engineered Biosystems Building (2012). (Courtesy of the Georgia Institute of Technology.)

The G. Wayne Clough Undergraduate Learning Commons opened in 2011 next to the library. At a cost of $93 million, it was a major investment for a non-dormitory student facility. It supplemented the nearby Skiles classroom building with an additional 41 classrooms, labs, study spaces, and two auditorium-style lecture halls. In keeping with the spirit of the times, it also included a large rooftop garden and a Starbucks coffee shop. (Courtesy of the Georgia Institute of Technology.)

Land clearing before the 1996 Olympics led to eastward expansion over the interstate in the 1990s. Tech purchased about 11 acres around Fifth Street and began planning for a university village envisioned by President Clough. Over time, Tech built a conference hotel, a conference center, a new College of Management (now the Scheller College), retail space, and parking. (Courtesy of the Georgia Institute of Technology.)

# *Two*

# TECH PEOPLE

In 1888, when Georgia Tech opened its doors for the first time, the combined student body, faculty, and staff barely exceeded 100 people. By 2018, that figure would exceed 30,000. As this chapter demonstrates—even though it can only scratch the surface in examining the many accomplished and notable individuals who have contributed to Georgia Tech—many administrators, faculty and staff, and students have played a significant role in the success of the institute.

As of 2018, Georgia Tech has had 11 presidents, who have served in the following order: Isaac S. Hopkins, Lyman Hall, Kenneth G. Matheson, Marion L. Brittain, Col. Blake R. Van Leer, Edwin D. Harrison, Arthur G. Hansen, Joseph M. Pettit, John Patrick Crecine, G. Wayne Clough, and G.P. "Bud" Peterson. Six other men have served as acting or interim president: Paul Weber, Vernon Crawford, James E. Boyd, Henry C. Bourne Jr., Michael E. Thomas, and Gary Schuster. Some significant Tech administrators have come from below the rank of president, among them George C. Griffin, who served as the dean of men from 1946 until 1964. Griffin was later memorialized with a statue outside the Ferst Center for the Arts, which students can often be seen posing next to for photographs.

During the 1950s and 1960s, as first women and then African Americans began to enter the ranks of Georgia Tech students and faculty, a number of relatively unsung women and men became important pioneers on campus, helping to pave the way for the much greater diversity that exists at Tech today. This chapter highlights some of those individuals, while others are featured in chapter three for playing a similar role on the athletic fields and courts of Georgia Tech.

Some faculty members have become very important in the history of Georgia Tech by virtue of having taught thousands of students over the course of several decades. While neither space nor the availability of photographs allows the inclusion of all of them, this chapter includes some who were perennial favorites among Tech students and whom many alumni should recall fondly.

A native of Monroe County, Georgia, John Fletcher Hanson (1840–1910) served in the Confederate army and later embarked on a successful business career with extensive interests in the textile, railroad, steamship, and newspaper publishing industries. In 1882, Hanson began publishing editorials in the *Macon Telegraph and Messenger* advocating for the establishment of a state technical institute of higher education, for which his biographer Lee Dunn calls him "the father of Georgia Tech."

A graduate of the University of Georgia, Nathaniel E. Harris (1846–1929) was working as a public attorney in Macon when he joined John Fletcher Hanson in the latter's crusade to create a state school of technology. Elected to the state legislature in 1882, Harris sponsored and shepherded the passage of the legislation that chartered the Georgia School of Technology in 1885. He later served a single term as governor of Georgia from 1915 to 1917.

Isaac Stiles Hopkins was president of Emory University in the 1880s when he was selected to be Tech's first president and head of the physics department in 1888. The 1920 General Catalog admitted that Tech made "small progress" during his years, although Hopkins did hire a number of professors who would make a great impact, such as John S. Coon and Lyman Hall. He resigned in 1895.

Lyman Hall (second row, third from left) was president from 1896 to 1905, during which time he added to Tech's limited curriculum in mechanical engineering by creating programs in textile engineering, electrical engineering, and chemistry (chemical engineering). He was particularly proud of the new program housed in the Textile Building, because he believed it would deal a direct blow to the near-monopoly in textile engineering held by Northern states. Fundraising for the chemistry building apparently affected his health, and he died in 1905.

Kenneth G. Matheson was elected president in 1906. His presidency was marked in later years by political battles and money shortages. However, he raised the money for the chemistry building and the YMCA and presided over the construction of the power plant and the mechanical engineering and military buildings, the Whitehead Hospital, and Grant Field. Frustrated and physically exhausted after fights over school funding, he resigned in 1921. Matheson is shown here at far right.

Marion L. Britain came to Georgia Tech in 1922 after being Georgia's superintendent of education for 12 years. One of his first priorities was getting Tech fully accredited, a major step in Tech's transition away from a mere trade school. Many of the notable buildings on campus were constructed in the Brittain era, often designed by architecture professors he brought to the school. Tech began granting graduate degrees during his tenure, which ended in 1944.

36

Blake R. Van Leer, president from 1944 to 1956, was an electrical and mechanical engineer who had served briefly in the Army, attaining the rank of colonel, "a title he preferred to any other," according to author Robert Wallace. Faced with budget shortfalls and a rapidly expanding student body, he struggled to grow the institute (the school became an institute in 1948) and expand research. Van Leer, shown here pointing, suffered a heart attack and died in 1956.

Edwin Harrison of the University of Toledo was hired as president in 1957. Harrison, the first Tech president to hold a doctorate, oversaw a remarkable expansion of the campus and the construction of the Skiles, Van Leer, and Bunger-Henry Buildings, the Wenn Student Center, the Radioisotopes and Bioengineering Building, the Neely Building, the Electronics Research Building, the Baker Building, the second Whitehead Infirmary, and five dormitories. He is pictured seated with his wife, Dorothy.

Arthur G. Hansen (1925–2010) had been a dean of engineering when he was nominated to succeed Edwin Harrison in 1969. Hansen reshuffled top administrative positions and led the acquisition of property near Hemphill Avenue under the guise of urban renewal, but then suddenly left to take another job in 1971. He is pictured at center in 1969.

Joseph M. Pettit (1916–1986) was hired as president in 1972. More than any previous president, Pettit elevated Tech's national stature as a modern research institution, increasing the research budget to more than $100 million for the first time, and also led a major fundraising campaign in 1985 that ultimately raised over $200 million. Pettit died in office from cancer in 1986. He is shown seated at left.

John P. "Pat" Crecine (1939–2008), president from 1987 to 1994, created new colleges of computing and science and reorganized the social sciences and management programs into the new Ivan Allen College. Crecine set out to make Georgia Tech into a full-fledged university and cleared a path to develop several new degree programs. In the late 1980s, Crecine participated in bringing the 1996 Olympic games to Atlanta. Crecine would not see those plans play out while still president; he resigned in 1994.

G. (Gerald) Wayne Clough (civil engineering class of 1964) replaced Crecine in 1994. He executed campus preparations for the Olympics and reorganized the Ivan Allen College with expanded non-engineering offerings. The campus in this period was extended, especially to the east and west, with the west campus dorms, the Erskine Manufacturing Building, graduate housing, Technology Square, the Petit Building, a new Whitehead Health Center, the Klaus Computing Building, the Nanotechnology Research Center, and others. Dr. Clough resigned in 2008.

In 2009, G.P. "Bud" Peterson became the 11th president of the Georgia Institute of Technology. Before he came to Tech, he served as the provost at Rensselaer Polytechnic Institute in Troy, New York, and as the chancellor at the University of Colorado at Boulder. He earned a doctorate in mechanical engineering at Texas A&M University, and in 2008, he was selected by Pres. George W. Bush to serve on the National Science Board. (Courtesy of the Georgia Institute of Technology.)

John "Uncle Heinie" Henika (1855–1951) is seen here, uncharacteristically in a suit under his shop apron. Uncle Heinie served as superintendent of the woodshop for over 60 years and was one of the best-known characters of Tech's early history. He died in 1951 at the age of 95, and the ANAK Society (see page 108) helped sponsor a portrait that was hung in the then-new Price Gilbert Library. (Courtesy of the Georgia Tech *Blueprint*.)

William V. Skiles, after whom the classroom building is named, first taught at Tech in 1906 in the mathematics department. As a dean in 1933, he created a research institution, eventually called the Engineering Experiment Station (now the Georgia Tech Research Institute). The *Blueprint* staff in 1935 called him "kindly, learned, austere, and possessed of the dignified reserve of a scholar and the sympathetic geniality of a gentleman." He retired in 1945.

Georgia Tech's own architecture professors, particularly Harold Bush-Brown, James Skinner, J.H. "Doc" Gailey, Kenneth K. Stowell, and later P.M. Heffernan, among others, designed Brown, Harris, and Cloudman Dormitories, Brittain Hall, the Guggenheim Building, the Naval Armory, the Old Gymnasium, Hightower Textile Building, the Hinman Building, the Price Gilbert Library, the Architecture Building, the Skiles Building, and others. Those pictured here include Harris (first row, left), Bush-Brown (first row, center), Gailey (first row, right), and Heffernan (fourth row, right).

Freddy Lanoue was a coach who in the 1930s developed a method of surviving long periods in water. His subsurface floating was so successful that by 1940, Georgia Tech mandated a drownproofing course for all students. Swimmers had their hands and sometimes their feet tied, but most were capable of remaining in the water for many hours. Students hated the course, but it was required through 1986. (Courtesy of the Georgia Tech *Blueprint*.)

George C. Griffin (1897–1990) taught mathematics beginning in 1930 and moved to an appointment as the dean of men in 1946, a position he held through 1964. Griffin oversaw student organizations, mentored students, and bailed pranksters out of jail on occasion. Among his other accomplishments, he served as track coach, and Tech honored his service in 1973 by naming the George Griffin Pi Mile Race.

Dean James Dull (1928–2009) came to Georgia Tech in 1957 as an assistant dean. Over the years, his work included preparing the institute for integration; overseeing student publications, fraternity matters, and disciplinary actions; and even organizing the Wreckettes drill team. He is responsible for purchasing the Ramblin' Wreck and creating the mascot Buzz. He is shown here at far right in the first row.

Paul G. Mayer (1923–1985) came to the United States in 1947 as a refugee from Frankfurt, Germany. He was a half-Jewish Holocaust survivor who spoke little English and possessed no money. In 1959, he joined the Tech faculty as a civil engineering professor. In 1974, he earned the distinction of being appointed a Regents Professor, and in 1985 he retired from Georgia Tech. A memorial garden on campus is named in his honor.

43

Patrick Kelly earned a doctorate in philosophy from Emory University in 1966 and then joined the faculty at Georgia Tech. He soon became the head of the Department of Social Sciences. He held that position for many years and played an important role in merging liberal arts and technology studies at Tech. He remained on the faculty into the 1990s.

Historian Robert C. McMath (born 1944) was hired by the social science department in 1972. There, he was one of a small group who taught US history, which (since 1954) has been required for graduation and thus been very popular. As the 1985 centennial of the institute approached, he and five colleagues wrote a history of the school. McMath rose to the position of vice provost before leaving in 2005. With him here is political science professor Dorothy Yancy. (Courtesy of the Georgia Tech *Blueprint*.)

There were no women in the fulltime regular faculty until 1968. Helen Grenga came to Tech as a postdoctoral fellow in chemistry in 1967. She was later offered a permanent position and stayed at Tech for the rest of her career. Eventually, she moved into the administration as director of the Office of Graduate Studies and Research and later became the dean of the Office of Academic Affairs. She died in 2006.

Philip Adler came to Tech in 1962 while still a doctoral candidate. He used the Socratic method of teaching and often assigned no textbooks. He was known for giving just one high-stakes examination, putting students into a stressful all-or-nothing situation. He put students on the spot in every class session, sometimes giving them extra assignments if they were too slow to answer. He retired in 2000.

Bill Leahy taught introductory computer science in 2000 as a master's student and recalled that his teaching style changed radically for the better after he happened to take a comedy improvisation class. After that, he found it easier to make connections with the students and keep them interested. His reputation as an instructor soared, and he kept what had been a temporary job until his retirement in 2017.

Economics professor William A. Schaffer joined the Georgia Tech faculty in 1964. He went on to teach Tech students for the next half-century, establishing a record for longevity that very few Tech faculty members have matched. A favorite among students, Schaffer received the Faculty of the Year award from the Student Government Association. He is shown receiving an award from Dean Jacqueline Jones Royster of the Ivan Allen College of Liberal Arts. (Courtesy of the Ivan Allen College of Liberal Arts, Georgia Institute of Technology.)

Jacqueline Jones Royster graduated from Spelman College in Atlanta and went on to earn master's and doctorate degrees in English from the University of Michigan. She became senior vice provost and executive dean of the Colleges of Arts and Sciences at the Ohio State University, and in 2010, she became the dean of the Ivan Allen College of Liberal Arts at Georgia Tech, making her the first African American dean in Tech's history. (Courtesy of the Ivan Allen College of Liberal Arts, Georgia Institute of Technology.)

Henry L. Smith (mechanical engineering, class of 1890) was the first graduate of Georgia Tech and one of just two students to graduate that year. Smith died in 1957. A coin toss allegedly determined that Smith's classmate George G. Crawford would be the second to graduate. Crawford became president of the Tennessee Coal, Iron, and Railroad Company and remained in the iron and steel industry until his death in 1936.

Racial integration was accomplished relatively easily in 1961 with the admission of three African American students, all from Atlanta: Ford Green, Ralph Long Jr., and Lawrence Williams. However, it was Ronald Yancey, a student admitted the next year, who became Tech's first African American graduate.

Tech students were for many years predominantly male. The commerce school started admitting women in 1917, and the first to graduate was Anna T. Wise, who later taught at the school. When the commerce school was transferred to the University of Georgia in 1933, there were no more women enrolled at Tech (except for night-school students) until 1952, when women were admitted on the main campus. While they could enroll in any academic program, they were not deemed eligible to attain all degrees in many of those programs until 1967. One of the first to enroll in 1952 was Barbara Michel. She and Shirley Clements (electrical engineering, class of 1956), a transfer student who enrolled later, were the first two women to graduate. Clements (now Shirley Clements Mewborn) is shown at left.

# *Three*

# SPORTS

The history of sports at Georgia Tech dates back to the institute's earliest days. Georgia Tech formed its first baseball team in 1889, less than half a year after the first Tech students began classes. Georgia Tech football started in the fall of 1892; the team's opponents that season included the University of North Carolina, the University of Virginia, Vanderbilt, Alabama A&M (Auburn), and Mercer University. By the time that Georgia Tech first met the University of Georgia on the gridiron on November 4, 1893, in Athens, the two colleges were already rivals on the baseball field. Football, however, became the primary focus of the rivalry of "clean, old-fashioned hate" between the two Georgia colleges that still endures in the 21st century. (Details about that 1893 game and a photograph of the Georgia Tech team follow in this chapter.) In the century and a quarter since Georgia Tech began playing football, the team has won four national championships: 1917, 1928, 1952, and 1990.

While Georgia Tech's teams have long been famously known as the Yellow Jackets, that was not always the case. The team that traveled to Athens in November 1893 was referred to in newspaper reports as simply "the Techs." Another early nickname for Georgia Tech teams was the Engineers. Some newspaper reports from 1902 to 1904 use the name "Blacksmiths," which apparently originated with sportswriters. "Yellowjackets"—as one word—first appeared in the *Atlanta Constitution* in 1905, but it did not catch on quickly. In 1917, when coach John Heisman led the football team to a perfect 9-0 championship season, sportswriters dubbed the team the "Golden Tornado," and that nickname stuck at least throughout the 1920s. Not until the 1930s did the name Yellow Jackets, which had reportedly been favored by Heisman, finally stick.

Georgia Tech sports programs expanded throughout the 20th century and for women in particular after Pres. Richard M. Nixon signed Title IX of the Education Amendments of 1972. Currently, Georgia Tech's NCAA Division I athletics program includes 17 men's and women's sports.

The rivalry of "clean, old-fashioned hate" between the Georgia Tech Yellow Jackets and the Georgia Bulldogs began when the two schools first met on the gridiron in Athens on November 4, 1893. Georgia Tech won that game 28-6. Leonard Wood (far right, reclining on the ground) scored the first touchdown. He later served as the commander of the 1st US Volunteer Cavalry (the "Rough Riders"), alongside his friend Theodore Roosevelt, in the Spanish-American War.

Many people would undoubtedly be surprised to learn that Georgia Tech had a baseball team before it had a football team. Articles in the *Atlanta Constitution* in March 1889 report on Tech baseball games. Here is the 1896 baseball team. The name of the coach is not known.

John Heisman, shown during the 1910s, left his job as head football coach at Clemson University in 1904 to take the helm at Georgia Tech. In 16 seasons, he compiled a record of 102-29-7. He also served as the head baseball coach, athletic director, and, intermittently, head basketball coach during his years at Georgia Tech. Since 1936, the Heisman Trophy has been awarded annually to the nation's top college football player.

In the most lopsided game in the history of college football, Georgia Tech defeated Cumberland (Tennessee) College by a score of 222-0 at Grant Field on October 7, 1916. Cumberland had disbanded its football team earlier in the year and sent a ragtag team to meet a contractual obligation. Coach Heisman ran up the score because he believed that Cumberland had used professionals in an earlier 22-0 victory over Tech in baseball.

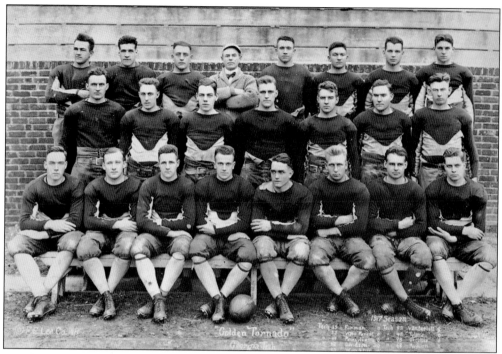

Coach Heisman's football team posted a nearly perfect record from 1915 through 1917, winning every game with the exception of two ties. The 1917 team, pictured here, won all nine games it played, including a 68-7 victory against Auburn on Thanksgiving Day, en route to winning the school's first national championship.

Joe Guyon played for Georgia Tech during 1917 and 1918. A member of the Chippewa tribe, he was born on the White Earth Indian Reservation in Minnesota. He played halfback as well as tackle, and in 1918, he won All-American honors at the latter position. He then went on to play professionally, and in 1966, he became the first man who had played for Georgia Tech to be inducted into the Pro Football Hall of Fame.

William A. "Bill" Alexander earned a degree in civil engineering, played football, and served under John Heisman as an assistant football coach at Georgia Tech. After serving in World War I in France, he became Tech's head basketball coach from 1919 until 1924, and head football coach from 1920 until 1944. In 1930, he helped form the Yellow Jacket Club, which later became the Ramblin' Reck Club. This photograph was taken around 1920.

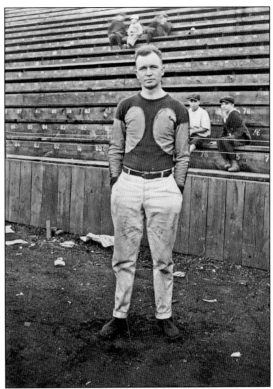

Student athletes have participated in track and field at Georgia Tech since 1904. Football coach John Heisman also coached the track and field team from its inception through 1908. This photograph was taken at the start of a 100-yard dash in 1920. Behind the runners is the Knowles Dormitory. Built in 1897, Knowles was located across from the Carnegie Building, and was demolished in 1992 to make space for the Bill Moore Student Success Center.

Georgia Tech won the 1928 national college football championship, the second in the school's history, upon defeating California by a score of 8-7 in the Rose Bowl on New Year's Day 1929. The margin of victory came in the form of a safety scored by Tech when California center Roy "Wrong Way" Riegels ran 65 yards in the wrong direction after recovering a fumble by Tech halfback John Griffin "Stumpy" Thomason.

Bobby Dodd (1908–1988) starred as a quarterback at the University of Tennessee from 1928 to 1930. He joined Georgia Tech as an assistant football coach in December 1930, and in 1945, he became the head coach. He held that position for 22 seasons and led the team to the national championship in 1952. He retired after the 1966 season with a record of 165-64-8. In 1988, Grant Field was renamed Bobby Dodd Stadium at Historic Grant Field.

Carl Waits (left), captain of the 1937 baseball team, is one of several Yellow Jackets who hold a team record for hitting two triples in one game. Next to him are an unidentified player and Bill McHenney (right). Bobby Dodd, an assistant football coach at the time, was the head coach of the baseball team from 1932 through 1939, except in 1936, when Tech did not field a baseball team.

Since Georgia Tech's student body consisted entirely of males prior to 1952, all of the cheerleaders were male as well. This photograph, taken at Grant Field in either 1939 or 1940, shows five unidentified cheerleaders.

*The Ramblin Reck of Georgia Tech*

*Halfback Clint Castleberry - Georgia Tech 1942*

By the time this undated photograph was taken, the composition of the cheerleading squad had changed considerably. As the Ramblin' Wreck rolled onto the field for a football game against the archrival Georgia Bulldogs (note the "To Hell with Georgia" flag on the front bumper), all of the cheerleaders standing on the running boards or in the rumble seat were women.

An Atlanta native, Clint Castleberry starred as a halfback for the Yellow Jackets in 1942 as a 19-year-old freshman. He finished third place in the voting for the Heisman Trophy. In February 1943, he was one of 18 Georgia Tech football players to be drafted into the Army Air Corps. Castleberry was killed in Liberia in November 1944 while piloting a B-26 bomber.

On December 28, 1952, the Yellow Jackets football team boarded a flight for New Orleans. There the Jackets would play in the Sugar Bowl at Tulane Stadium on New Year's Day 1953, defeating the Ole Miss Rebels by the score of 24-7. This victory concluded a perfect 12-0 season that resulted in Georgia Tech being named the 1952 season national champions in the International News Service poll.

Offensive tackle Hal Miller was an All-American and the co-captain of the 1952 national championship team. Miller played for the San Francisco 49ers in 1953 before entering the US Army. In 1992, he became a member of the Georgia Tech Athletic Hall of Fame. Posing with him here is 1953 Miss America Neva Jane Langley of Macon.

This seat cushion commemorates the Sugar Bowl in which the Yellow Jackets clinched their national championship for the 1952 season. This side of the cushion is yellow (not gold) and shows Tulane Stadium, the annual home of the Sugar Bowl during that era. The other side is striped.

Atlanta native Larry Morris served as captain of the Yellow Jackets football and baseball teams. In football, he played both center and linebacker and won All-American honors in 1953. In the NFL, he played for the Los Angeles Rams, Chicago Bears, and Atlanta Falcons, primarily as a linebacker. While playing for the Bears, he was named the MVP of the 1963 NFL championship game.

Georgia governor Marvin Griffin tried to keep the Yellow Jackets out of the 1956 Sugar Bowl because the other team, the University of Pittsburgh Panthers, had an African American player. In response, Georgia Tech students marched upon the state capitol and, as seen here, the governor's mansion in protest. Georgia Tech defeated Pitt by a score of 7-0 on January 2, 1956, in New Orleans.

In 1999, Billy Shaw became the second (and as of this writing, most recent) former Georgia Tech player to be inducted into the Pro Football Hall of Fame. An All-American two-way tackle at Tech, he played for nine seasons as an offensive guard for the Buffalo Bills, then of the AFL, and was an All-Star eight of those seasons. He played for Georgia Tech from 1958 to 1960.

In what most alumni of the two institutions would probably consider a case of fraternizing with the enemy, alumni of the Georgia Tech and University of Georgia cross-country teams met for a joint reunion in 1958. Seated second from left is George C. Griffin (civil engineering, class of 1922), who served as Georgia Tech's dean of students from 1946 until his retirement in 1964.

Sam Nunn attended Georgia Tech from 1956 to 1959. He then transferred to Emory University, graduating in 1961 and earning a law degree there in 1962. He represented Georgia in the US Senate from 1972 until 1997. Since then, he has been a distinguished professor at Georgia Tech's Sam Nunn School of International Affairs. Here he is shown as a member of the varsity golf team in 1959.

Born in Lula, Georgia, in 1912, John "Whack" Hyder lettered in baseball, basketball, track, and cross-country at Georgia Tech during the 1930s. After playing minor-league baseball and serving in World War II, he returned to Tech as an assistant basketball coach. From 1951 to 1973, he was the head coach, and he is a member of the Georgia Tech Athletics Hall of Fame as both a basketball player and coach.

Pictured here are Georgia Tech football radio announcers Al Ciraldo (left) and Jack Hurst. Hurst called Yellow Jackets games from 1959 until 1964 and later became one of the first members of the Atlanta Falcons radio broadcast team. Ciraldo called 416 Tech football games and 1,030 basketball games from 1954 until 1992, and was posthumously inducted into the Georgia Radio Hall of Fame and the Atlanta Sports Hall of Fame.

The Georgia Tech tennis team won the Southeastern Conference (SEC) championship in 1960. Georgia Tech helped found the SEC in 1932, but in 1964, Bobby Dodd and Tech president Edwin Harrison withdrew the institute from the conference. Tech competed independently in athletics for a decade, helped found the Metro Conference in 1975, and finally joined the Atlantic Coast Conference (ACC) in 1979.

Jim Luck played football at Georgia Tech and earned a degree in industrial management in 1948. In 1955, he became a member of coach Bobby Dodd's football staff, but switched to the baseball program and became the head coach in 1962. He soon led the baseball team to prominence, finishing the 1965 season ranked eighth nationally. He served as head coach for 20 seasons.

Although he looks like a kicker or punter here, Billy Lothridge was the first-string quarterback as well as captain of the 1963 Yellow Jackets. He was also the runner-up to future Dallas Cowboys superstar Roger Staubach for the Heisman Trophy that year. This photograph foreshadowed his nine-season NFL career (mostly as a member of the Atlanta Falcons), during which his primary position was punter.

North Augusta (South Carolina) High School graduate Jerry Priestly lettered in three sports at Georgia Tech during the early to mid-1960s—baseball, basketball, and as seen here, football. He was the Yellow Jackets' first-string quarterback in 1964, and the following year, he was the backup to Kim King. In 1982, he was inducted into the Georgia Tech Athletics Hall of Fame.

This posed photograph from 1966 shows quarterback Kim King and running back Lenny Snow. King went on to spend three decades as a broadcaster calling Yellow Jackets football games while also becoming a successful commercial real estate developer. Just before his death in October 2004, Georgia Tech honored him by dedicating the Kim King Football Locker Room at Bobby Dodd Stadium at Historic Grant Field.

In 1970, Eddie McAshan broke the color line not only as the first African American to play football for the Yellow Jackets but also as the first to become a starting quarterback at any major college in the Southeast. McAshan earned a degree in industrial management, and in 1995, was inducted into the Georgia Tech Athletics Hall of Fame.

This photograph, most likely taken in 1976, shows Bobby Dodd with Bill Curry. Curry played center for Dodd's teams from 1962 to 1964, and followed that with a 10-year playing career in the NFL. In 1976, Curry returned to Georgia Tech as an assistant coach for one season, and later served as head coach from 1980 to 1986. He has also served as head coach at Alabama, Kentucky, and Georgia State.

The Georgia Tech Rugby Football Club began in 1975. The Georgia Tech Women's Rugby Football Club began 31 years later. Both teams play during the fall and spring semesters, and the men's team plays during the summer semester as well. Shown here is the men's team in 1988.

An All-American quarterback at Centre College, Homer Rice had a long career as a football coach for high school and college teams as well as the NFL's Cincinnati Bengals. He became Georgia Tech's athletics director in 1980 and held that post until his retirement in 1997. He has remained an active member of the Georgia Tech community, and facilities in Bobby Dodd Stadium as well as the Price Gilbert Library are named in his honor.

Bobby Cremins served as head coach of the men's basketball team from 1981 until 2000. Cremins retired from the post with a record of 354-237, and led the Yellow Jackets to nine consecutive appearances in the NCAA tournament beginning in 1984–1985. He subsequently held the position of head coach at the College of Charleston from 2006 to 2012. The basketball court at McCamish Pavilion is named Cremins Court in his honor.

Bernadette McGlade was Georgia Tech's first full-time female head coach when she became the women's basketball coach in 1981. She held that position for seven seasons and also served as the women's sports coordinator and senior associate athletic director during her 16 years at Georgia Tech. In 2012, she was chosen as a Yellow Jackets ACC Legend.

Agnus Berenato succeeded her sister, Bernadette McGlade, as Georgia Tech's women's basketball head coach in 1988. In 15 seasons, she compiled a record of 223-209. In 1992, she led the Yellow Jackets to their first championship in the National Women's Invitational Tournament. Here she is shown removing the net following that victory.

Mark Price played as a guard for the Yellow Jackets from 1982 to 1986. He went on to have an outstanding career in the National Basketball Association, playing for 12 seasons and being selected as an All-Star four times. He returned to Georgia Tech for a year as an assistant coach in 1999, and in 2013, he was chosen as an ACC Legend. (Courtesy of the Georgia Tech Athletic Association.)

A star for the Yellow Jackets from 1982 to 1986, John Salley is one of only 10 Georgia Tech student athletes to have his jersey number retired. The 6-foot-11-inch power forward and center later became the first player in NBA history to win championships with three different teams, as well as the first to win a championship in three different decades. (Courtesy of the Georgia Tech Athletic Association.)

Kevin Brown came to Georgia Tech as a shortstop but became a pitcher instead. He helped the team win ACC championships in 1985 and 1986, and later in 1986, he made his major-league debut for the Texas Rangers. In his 17 seasons as a big-league pitcher, he compiled a 211-144 record with a 3.28 earned run average. He was also a six-time All-Star. (Courtesy of the Georgia Tech Athletic Association.)

Georgia Tech's women's volleyball team played its inaugural season in 1980. Shelton Collier became the head coach in 1991, and during his 11 seasons, the team won its first ACC tournament championship in 1995 and also finished the season as ACC regular-season champion in 1994, 1995, and 2000. This photograph was taken during a game in or around 2000.

The 1989–1990 men's basketball team became Georgia Tech's first to advance to the NCAA Final Four. Shown here are guard Karl Brown (5) and forward Johnny McNeil (24) following the team's victory over Minnesota at the Superdome in New Orleans on March 25, 1990, which earned the Yellow Jackets their Final Four berth.

Dennis Scott, the 1989–1990 ACC and Sporting News Player of the Year, led Georgia Tech to its first appearance in the NCAA Final Four in 1990. He then left to enter the NBA draft, where he was selected as the fourth pick by the Orlando Magic. The 6-foot-8-inch small forward became known as one of the game's greatest three-point shooters. (Courtesy of the Georgia Tech Athletic Association.)

David Duval was a four-time All-American golfer at Georgia Tech, two-time ACC Player of the Year, and the 1993 National Player of the Year. In 1999, he achieved the number one position in the Official World Golf Ranking. In 2003, he was inducted into the Georgia Tech Athletics Hall of Fame. (Courtesy of the Georgia Tech Athletic Association.)

After defeating the Nebraska Cornhuskers 45-21 in the Citrus Bowl in Orlando on New Year's Day 1991, the Georgia Tech Yellow Jackets were named the 1990 season national champions by the UPI Poll. Here, head coach Bobby Ross is hoisted by James Reese (44) and Marty Quinn (64).

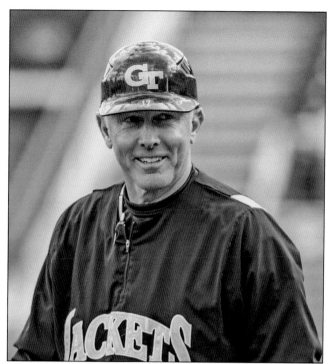

Danny Hall played baseball at Miami (Ohio) University from 1974 to 1977. In 1978, he became an assistant baseball coach at his alma mater, beginning a career that would lead him to Georgia Tech as the head baseball coach in 1994. He still holds that position in 2018, and has become the winningest and longest-serving coach in the program's history. (Courtesy of the Georgia Tech Athletic Association and Danny Karnik.)

In 1994, the Yellow Jackets made their first appearance in the College World Series. The player receiving high-fives from his teammates, Nomar Garciaparra (5), went on to have a stellar career in the major leagues. He won the American League Rookie of the Year Award in 1997 and finished his 14-year career with a .313 lifetime batting average. In 2004, he was inducted into the Georgia Tech Hall of Fame.

Catcher Jason Varitek (33), shown in the 1994 NCAA tournament, was a teammate of Nomar Garciaparra not only at Georgia Tech but later with the Boston Red Sox as well. Varitek played for the Red Sox from 1997 to 2011. He made the American League All-Star team three times, and won a Gold Glove Award in 2005.

During his four seasons as a Yellow Jacket (1994–1997), linebacker Keith Brooking became the leading tackler in Georgia Tech history. The Atlanta Falcons chose him in the first round of the 1998 NFL draft, and he played for the Falcons for the first 11 of his 15 seasons in the NFL. He was selected to the Pro Bowl five times as a Falcon. (Courtesy of the Georgia Tech Athletic Association.)

When Atlanta hosted the 1996 Olympics, Georgia Tech served as the home of the Olympic Village (where the athletes were housed) as well as the site for boxing, diving, modern pentathlon, Paralympic volleyball, swimming, synchronized swimming, and water polo. Artist Richard Hill designed the 80-foot Kessler Campanile, named for alumnus Richard C. Kessler and built for the Olympics.

Powerful switch-hitting third baseman Mark Teixeira was one of the greatest baseball players in Georgia Tech history. He was the 1999 ACC Rookie of the Year, 2000 ACC Player of the Year, and winner of the Dick Howser Trophy in 2000 as the national college player of the year. He switched to first base as a major leaguer, winning five Gold Gloves and hitting 409 home runs in 14 seasons. (Courtesy of the Georgia Tech Athletic Association.)

Wide receiver Calvin Johnson won a long list of honors during his three seasons as a Yellow Jacket, including ACC Player of the Year in 2006. From 2007 to 2015, he had an outstanding career with the Detroit Lions, being selected to the Pro Bowl six times and named First-Team All-Pro three times. In 2018, Johnson was inducted into the College Football Hall of Fame. (Courtesy of the Georgia Tech Athletic Association.)

Singapore native Jaime Wong played tennis at Georgia Tech from 2000 to 2003, setting team records for victories in singles (101) and doubles (82) matches. In 2002, she became the first Tech tennis player ever to be selected to compete in the NCAA Women's Tennis Singles Championship, and she was chosen the following year as well. In 2016, she was inducted into the Georgia Tech Hall of Fame. (Courtesy of the Georgia Tech Athletic Association.)

In 1913, Atlanta businessman John W. Grant donated $15,000 to build a football stadium, which was named Hugh Inman Grant Field after his deceased son. Convict labor played a role in its construction. Expanded and remodeled numerous times, the stadium is now named Bobby Dodd Stadium at Historic Grant Field. This photograph, taken looking east, dates from the 1960s or 1970s.

Named after Tech's legendary football and basketball coach William Alexander, the Alexander Memorial Coliseum was the home of Georgia Tech basketball from 1956 until 2011. Nicknamed "the Thrillerdome" by Tech basketball radio announcer Brad Nessler during the 1983–1984 season, the coliseum was renamed the McCamish Pavilion after undergoing extensive renovation during 2011 and 2012. This photograph dates from either the late 1960s or the 1970s.

# *Four*

# STUDENT LIFE

In 1888, Atlanta was a much smaller city than it is today; the 1890 US Census reported its population as 65,533. The massive suburban sprawl that Atlanta is famous (or infamous) for now did not develop until the latter half of the 20th century, spurred by the Baby Boom, post–World War II prosperity, the construction of interstate highways, and, on a less positive note, "white flight" out of the city during and after the civil rights movement of the 1950s and 1960s. Considering that North Avenue marked, as the name implies, the northern end of the city limits during the early decades of Atlanta's existence, it is clear that the city offered Georgia Tech students far fewer opportunities for entertainment and recreation than it does currently.

As examined in chapter three, sports quickly came to provide a recreational outlet for the student body. Fraternities would soon follow, as covered in chapter five. Tech students also created a plethora of campus traditions, some of which still exist today, such as the Freshman Cake Race and the Ramblin' Wreck Parade. By the end of the Roaring Twenties, two cultural landmarks that still exist near the campus today, the Varsity restaurant and the Fox Theater, had both opened. The founder of the Varsity, Frank Gordy, attended Georgia Tech during the mid-1920s.

Student life at Georgia Tech changed considerably beginning in the 1950s. Female students enrolled starting in the fall of 1952, followed by African Americans nine years later, and the campus became remarkably diverse by the beginning of the 21st century. The Fred B. Wenn Student Center opened in 1970, providing students with, among other amenities, a bowling alley and a pool hall. The aquatic center constructed on campus for the 1996 Olympics subsequently became an outstanding facility for the use of students (as well as faculty and staff). Furthermore, the metropolitan Atlanta area has become one of the nation's 10 largest, offering Tech students a wealth of opportunities for entertainment and recreation off campus.

The Whistle of
Georgia Tech
until 1995

*Presented to*

**PRESIDENT CLOUGH**

IN HONOR OF HIS INAUGURATION

*By the Class of 1995*

The famous steam whistle was originally installed on the Shop Building. Historians believe the whistle was chosen instead of a bell to mark the time because it was reminiscent of the factory whistles that began and ended the workday. In 1905, the whistle was stolen for the first of many times. Originally, the culprits were students from archrival University of Georgia, but later, Tech students themselves began stealing it, leading to the imposition of a 10¢ fine on every student each time it was stolen. Eventually relocated to the power plant building, it has served for many decades despite the thefts. The most famous heist in recent decades was in 1995. During the inaugural parade for Pres. G. Wayne Clough, which was to be announced by the blowing of the whistle, it was seized by pranksters, who later presented the stolen brass icon to him as a gift.

Georgia Tech's fight song, "Ramblin' Wreck from Georgia Tech," has a controversial and confusing history. The music was based on an old British folk song called "The Son of a Gambolier," which included the line "I'm a rambling wretch of poverty." A new variation of that song was published in 1895 and somehow made its way to Tech. That version substituted the words "rambling rake" for "rambling wretch," which may be the inspiration for "ramblin' wreck." A student in the 1890s claimed, decades later, that classmate Billy Walthall wrote the words to create the current fight song. While there were numerous variations of "Ramblin' Wreck," Tech's early band director, Frank Roman, had the words and music published in the 1920s, which had the effect of standardizing the lyrics in more or less their current form. "Ramblin' Wreck" is one of the most famous college fight songs ever, having been recorded dozens of times since the first Columbia Record Company issue of 1925.

The sharing of a meal is one of the great college traditions. Several of Tech's early dormitories, such as Knowles, built in 1897, had their own dining rooms, and the college offered an optional meal plan. Undoubtedly the most important of Tech's dining facilities is Brittain Hall, shown here, with its elaborate architecture and stained-glass windows. Sideways the dog was said to be a regular visitor during her short stay on campus (see page 87).

The College Inn and Bookstore was opened in an attempt to lure students away from shops on Cherry Street that sold alcohol. Originally called the Ramble Inn, it was opened in 1925 in the lower level of the Administration Building after the physics department moved to its new building down the street. At some point, the name was changed to the College Inn, but it was informally known as the "Robbery." There is some uncertainty as to when the College Inn closed, but it was made redundant by the opening of the Wynn Student Center in 1970 and was closed for business by the time of the dedication of the Georgia Tech bookstore in 1971. (Courtesy of the Georgia Tech *Blueprint*.)

The tradition of building Ramblin' Wrecks began in 1929, when the first Atlanta-to-Athens road race was held. In part for safety reasons, the event was converted to a parade in 1932, featuring classic cars, specially decorated vehicles, and student-built contraptions, the wackier the better. The Ramblin' Wreck Parade is not to be confused with the Ramblin' Wreck, the restored Ford Model A owned by the institute. The photograph above shows an unidentified entrant in the 1962 "contraptions" category.

The Varsity restaurant was originally the Yellow Jacket, located at Hemphill Avenue and Luckie Street, but relocated to its present location at North and Spring Streets early in its history. The Varsity has always catered to local Tech students, but became the "World's Largest Drive-In" by encouraging diners from all over with ample parking and curb service (service to one's automobile). Despite losing part of its parking to the expansion of Interstate 75/85, and shifting consumer tastes, the Varsity soldiers on as one of the area's oldest surviving business establishments. (Courtesy of Tracy O'Neal Photographic Collection, Special Collections and Archives, Georgia State University Library.)

Coach Bill Alexander had pushed for expanding intramural sports since the 1920s, but the program took on new importance after the purchase of a large lot along Fowler Street between Fifth and Eighth Streets. Most of the $80,000 funding came from winnings for the 1929 Rose Bowl game in California, so the area became known as Rose Bowl Field. Baseball and practice football games were held there as well as ROTC exercises, Field Day, and various intramural sports events. Most of the open space has been gradually taken by construction of sports facilities.

| CHECK ONE | PART TIME | | GEORGIA RESIDENT | NON RESIDENT |
|---|---|---|---|---|
| | 1 thru 5 hours | 6 thru 11 hours | | |
| Matriculation @ $14.00/hr. | | | $168.00 | $168.00 |
| Tuition @ $29.50/hr. | | | | 354.00 |
| Transportation Fee | 2.50 | 2.50 | 2.50 | 2.50 |
| Student Activity ✳ | | 18.00 | 18.00 | 18.00 |
| Health Service ✳ | | 20.00 | 20.00 | 20.00 |
| Total Fees | | | $208.50 | $562.50 |
| Total Hours | | | | |

**FEE CARD**

COLLECTIONS' COPY

GEORGIA INSTITUTE OF TECHNOLOGY
ATLANTA, GEORGIA 30332

**WINTER QTR. 1976**

Cashier's Stamp

✳ These fees are mandatory for Part Time Students registering for at least six hours but less than 12. These fees are voluntary for less than six hours.

Name of Contract:_____

PART TIME STUDENTS FILL IN COLUMN 1 OR 2 IN ACCORDANCE WITH THE NUMBER OF HOURS YOU ARE TAKING. AUDIT COURSES ARE REQUIRED TO BE PAID AT REGULAR RATE.

Please do not fold, mark, or crumple this card.

---

The fictional George P. Burdell was the creation of alumnus William E. Smith in 1927. That first year, Burdell signed up for all the same classes that Smith had, turned in assignments and tests, and received grades. He lettered in football and earned his first degree, one of many. By 1930, Burdell as an alumnus remained active as both an undergraduate and graduate student. He fought simultaneously in both theaters of war in World War II, while at home, he became a noted writer of letters to the editor and was frequently paged at public events. In 1958, he married fictitious Agnes Scott student Ramona Cartwright. He was the bane of businesses both local and remote, ordering up insurance policies, mail order items, and once, a truckload of furniture, without a thought of paying for any of it. He once bought a long-running subscription to *Playboy* magazine for Dean Jim Dull. And he famously enrolled for every single class the first term that Tech used its new computerized registration system in 1969. Burdell continues to be one of Tech's great traditions.

WILLIAM EDGAR SMITH

AUGUSTA, GA.

Φ Σ Κ

*Ceramic Engineering*

American Ceramic Society.

One of Tech's oldest traditions is the Freshman Cake Race, first run in 1911. In the early years, the top finishers in this cross-country race got a cake as a prize. Originally intended to support the cross-country team, it officially became a freshmen-only event in 1935. It was eventually linked to Homecoming festivities, and later, the winner also earned a kiss from the Homecoming queen.

During the several decades when Tech only admitted males, the amorous men of Tech found ways to bring women on campus, at least temporarily. For the innumerable dances, balls, football games, and other events, women were recruited from nearby colleges, in particular the equally deprived all-female Agnes Scott College. Even after the introduction of coeducation in 1952, the institute remained largely male. Tech's male-to-female ratio was 70:1 in the late 1960s and 5:1 in 1981. Today it is 1.7:1. (Courtesy of the Georgia Tech *Blueprint*.)

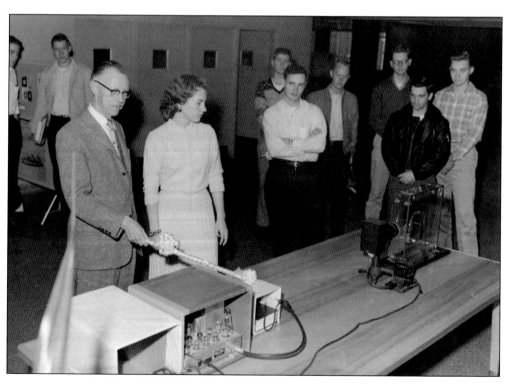

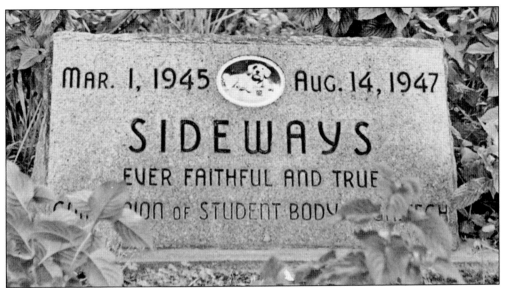

MAR. 1, 1945   AUG. 14, 1947
SIDEWAYS
EVER FAITHFUL AND TRUE
C.... ....ON OF STUDENT BODY ..... .... TECH

Campus pets, especially dogs, have been a major feature of campus life, and the most famous of these was Sideways. The little dog had a peculiar way of walking, thought to be the result of being hit by a car. According to legend, Sideways was owned by a woman living at North Avenue and Williams Street whose home was demolished. Though she moved, the dog returned to the area, and the woman asked students to adopt the dog. From 1945 to 1947, Sideways roamed the campus and its buildings freely, frequenting any classroom, lab, or dorm that looked like a good place for a meal or a nap. Her life and career have been honored with a granite marker near Tech Tower. Incidentally, she is not the only canine to be commemorated with a grave on campus: electrical engineering professor Daniel Fielder's dog, Socrates, is buried under a marker on the lawn of the Van Leer Building.

While the Ramblin' Wreck car race and at least one other Ramblin' Wreck predate it, the current Ramblin' Wreck automobile became official in 1961, when noted dean James Dull purchased the car from Ted Johnson, a Delta Air Lines pilot. Captain Johnson had restored the 1930 Ford Model A to "daily driver" condition over the course of several years. For many years, the car has led the football team onto the field at games and led the Homecoming procession.

Dormitory life today barely resembles the primitive conditions of years past. For instance, the small wooden dormitories known as the "Shacks," once located near Grant Field, lacked both electric lighting and indoor plumbing. Even late-20th-century dorms usually had dreary cinder block walls, and residents shared bedrooms and bathrooms. But old dorms were renovated and new dorms built on campus at a furious rate since the early 1990s. Even the old dorms were updated with amenities they had never enjoyed before, such as cable television hookups, while the new (more expensive) dorms attempted to match commercial apartments off-campus with such luxuries as private bedrooms, microwave ovens, and dishwashers. (Both, courtesy of the Georgia Tech *Blueprint*.)

Non-technical people probably know about scientific laboratories only from two Hollywood clichés: either the brightly-lit, sterile, orderly lab populated by people in white lab coats, or Dr. Frankenstein's darker lab, littered with open flames, arcing electric equipment, and experimental contrivances that look cobbled together. Tech students know from experience that the reality is closer to the Frankenstein model. Since the construction of the Shop Building and the chemistry labs in the Lyman Hall building, Tech has given students up-close access to the messy and often noisy, smelly, and chaotic world of real engineering science.

Millennials may not know that classroom "technology" used to consist entirely of a lecturer, a chalkboard, and an eraser. At a college like Tech, where lectures were more math- and science-intensive than the typical liberal arts institution, instructors also came to rely on advanced teaching technologies such as devices to project transparent slides onto a viewing screen. Students carried slide rules to make quick approximations of complex calculations, and the use of specialized slide rules was sometimes taught in class as well. (Both, courtesy of the Georgia Tech *Blueprint*.)

91

The road originally called Third Street and eventually renamed Bobby Dodd Way was for decades the main path between dormitories and classroom buildings. Freshman Hill is the steep stretch between about Fowler Street and the library. This photograph of the hill from the early 1970s is notable not only for the hoodless wreck of a Fiat in the foreground but also for the odd structure spanning the road at Fowler Street. (Both, courtesy of the Georgia Tech *Blueprint*.)

That odd structure was originally built to include a ticket booth for stadium events, but the booth itself was eventually removed. The *Blueprint* yearbook declared it a campus "monstrosity." It remained in place through the 1990s, when it was unceremoniously torn down during preparations for the 1996 Olympics.

The legendary Ramblin' Raft Race was one of Tech's greatest social events of the 1970s and was surely the best idea the brothers of Delta Sigma Phi (established at Tech in 1920) have ever had. The race, held yearly from 1969 to 1980, drew people from across the country and elevated fraternity-style debauchery to an international level years before *Animal House* was even a concept. Launched by Delta Sig Larry Patrick (textile engineering, class of 1973), it pitted profoundly drunken rafters against each other over a 10-mile stretch on the mostly slow-moving Chattahoochee. While most entrants floated around in old inner tubes, purpose-built "rafts" were a key feature (recalling the Ramblin' Wreck Parade), and some competitors went all-out. Delta Sigma Phi's 1970 entry, for example, was a 34-foot pirate ship with multiple decks and a mast, and fittingly, it sank due to the extreme drunkenness and pathetic navigation skills of the crew. The races drew tens of thousands, but the drinking, the noise, the nudity, the trash, and the abandoned vessels drew the ire of local residents, and after 1980, the event was scuttled. (Both, courtesy of the Georgia Tech *Blueprint*.)

The term "nerd" or "nurd" probably originated in the 1970s; a report on college slang in 1980 helped popularize the term as "a person dedicated to academics with little or no social life." The personality type certainly predated the term by many decades, and the *Technique* and the *Blueprint* over the years both reflect a sort of pride in being a nerd. Academics who studied the nerd phenomenon noted that self-described nerds were usually male and white, and that engineering education nurtured nerd-dom at the cost of creating an atmosphere inhospitable to women, non-whites, and others. By the 1990s, responding to the gradual opening of technical education to a more diverse student body, being a nerd had become less a source of shame than a badge of honor. (Both, courtesy of the Georgia Tech *Blueprint*.)

The "TECH" mounted on the tower of the Administration Building first appeared as smaller, wooden letters lighted from below and were donated by the class of 1922. The current signage, with metal frames and integral lighting, was installed around 1950 and featured prominently in the 1952 *Blueprint*. Stealing the T (and other letters) is a more recent tradition dating from 1969, when a group of fraternity men took down the T and presented it to the outgoing president. President Crecine, who called T-stealing one of Tech's great traditions, recounted waking up one morning to find a C in his front yard (for "Crecine"). The letters were welded in place beginning in the 1980s and penalties for theft stiffened. Most recently, a T stealer in 2014 was fined $14,000. (Courtesy of the Georgia Tech *Blueprint*.)

Georgia Tech students have never been known for their political activism, even in the divisive 1960s and 1970s. While students across the nation were occupying administration buildings and burning draft cards, Tech students held a demonstration in favor of the Vietnam War in 1968, then held Wonderful Ed's Day in 1969 in honor of Pres. Edwin Harrison. Following the Kent State tragedy in Ohio in 1970, students held a memorial rather than a protest. When social activism led many students to abandon fraternities and sororities, ROTC, and religious organizations, Greek membership declined only slightly at Tech in the 1960s and 1970s, and ROTC and religious institutions thrived. Despite the fact that Tech was up to its institutional eyeballs in military research by the late 1960s, no significant protests have ever been held against the Engineering Experiment Station (now GTRI). And by the 1990s, on the day of the outbreak of Operation Desert Storm in the Middle East, ROTC students marched on campus in favor of the war, unopposed (although many students joined an off-campus protest that night). (Courtesy of the Georgia Tech *Blueprint*.)

Drinking establishments serving the Georgia Tech community have a very long history dating back almost to the founding of the institution, although none of them had the longevity of restaurants such as the Varsity or the now-defunct Junior's. Still, from the late 1960s to the mid-1990s, there were a series of notorious dives, mostly along North Avenue and Marietta Street south of campus. These included One Eyed Jacks on North Avenue, famous for its Thursday beer specials, and a cluster of bars and bar-and-grill establishments near Cherry Street. Far too many beers were consumed at M.J. Pippins, K.G. Grumpy's, and Pero's, perhaps followed by cheap Chinese food from nearby Reckshaw's. Students willing to walk a bit farther found P.J. Haley's Nest (formerly Burdell's) on Marietta Street. (Both, courtesy of the Georgia Tech *Blueprint*.)

Originally located on North Avenue, the restaurant that became Junior's Grill first opened in 1948. James Klemis and John Chaknis bought that restaurant in 1958, changed its name to Junior's, and operated at several locations between 1967 and 1987. The final move came in 1994, when Junior's relocated to the Bradley Building on campus. Declining patronage led to Tommy Klemis, son of the first owner, closing the restaurant in 2011. Tommy Klemis is shown at right in 1978 making a bowl of glop. One of Junior's several locations, shown below, was next door to one of Engineer's Bookstore's several locations. (Both, courtesy of the Georgia Tech *Blueprint*.)

Tech holds no monopoly on student pranks, but there was something about the combination of young, immature minds and sophisticated engineering knowledge that encouraged many memorable stunts over the years. Highly exothermic chemical reactions, dangerously destructive computer code, and elaborate schemes to raise (or lower) heavy objects into places they clearly should not be were all popular prank themes. The repeated theft of the Tech T is treated elsewhere, but newspaper police blotters over the years recorded some of the best and most destructive stunts. Sadly, few were captured on film, but a humorous take on the Boggs building sign around 1979 is seen here. (Courtesy of the Georgia Tech *Blueprint*.)

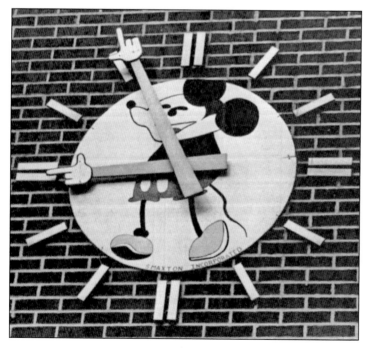

The (often non-functional) Mickey Mouse clock installed on Skiles was originally a prank by two graduating seniors, Lindsey Smith and Henry Claxton. As is so often the case with Tech pranks, the two left a clue: they added the "manufacturer's" name "Smaxton" in small letters at the bottom of the clock face. Hung in 1978, the prank clock was deemed harmless, even useful, so it remains to this day. (Courtesy of the Georgia Tech *Blueprint*.)

There has never been an era when parking on campus was easy, but before the 1990s, parking spaces were at least available in small numbers all over campus and often very close to dorms and class buildings. Relatively large faculty lots, for example, existed in the broad space between the library and the Van Leer/Architecture Buildings until the 2000s, when they began to be replaced with greenspace and the Clough Learning Center.

Photographs of the Tech campus from the 1910s and 1920s show well-manicured grounds, but with the sprawling growth of the post–World War II period, grounds maintenance fell behind. The 1975 *Blueprint* called out the "assorted monstrosities" on campus, such as the MARTA bus stop signs that had been defaced to read "FARTA." Despite several campus beautification programs, including the one that led to the installation of the famous campus fountain, it was not until preparations for the 1996 Olympics that the current, manicured look came to be. (Courtesy of the Georgia Tech *Blueprint*.)

From the start, fraternities and social clubs held dances and events with musical entertainment. But beginning around 1945 and accelerating in the 1960s, Tech began hosting more large-scale concerts where famous bands were featured. Between 1945 and 1948, for example, big band leaders Sammy Kaye, Les Brown, and Jimmy Dorsey, along with singer and movie star Doris Day, put on memorable shows. The expanded football stadium and the new Alexander Coliseum made really large rock concerts on campus possible, drawing crowds from far outside Atlanta. A landmark was the Champagne Jam series in 1978 and 1979, multi-band festivals with many national rock acts. Notable performances included the Allman Brothers (1971), Foreigner (1977), Bob Seger (1977), Heart (1977), Kansas (1979), the Marshall Tucker Band (1981), Simon and Garfunkel (1984), and the Rolling Stones (1989, 1994, and 2015). (Both, courtesy of the Georgia Tech *Blueprint*.)

Built after the construction of Interstate 75/85 threatened to cut off convenient access to midtown from North Campus, the Third Street tunnel has had a checkered career. Plagued by graffiti and public urination, it has also been, at times, notorious as a site of muggings. Only open now for football games and special events, equipped with semi-functional security cameras, and subject to special police patrols, the tunnel remains the ugliest way to enter or leave campus. (Courtesy of the Georgia Tech *Blueprint*.)

Among Tech's most frustrating requirements, the act of registering for classes has historically ranked near the top. Through the 1960s, registration was accomplished entirely by hand, resulting in long lines at the Old Gymnasium near Bobby Dodd Stadium. The process was gradually improved by computerization, first in 1969 and then again in 1982, but these systems still required hiking to a designated building and waiting in lines to register. The former gymnasium of the O'Keefe Building, located at the extreme north end of campus, was the last place used for in-person registration.

The Mini 500 tricycle race has its origins among the many degrading hazing rituals perfected at Tech by fraternities. Some of these groups would compel their pledges to ride around campus on tricycles. In 1969, the Ramblin' Reck Club formalized the activity, converting it into a race and making it part of the annual Homecoming events. Here, tube-socked and beer-shirted students push their way up the hill near Peters Park.

A fountain and sculpture installation near the library entrance was built in 1976 as part of a controversial campus beautification program. The $17,000 installation followed a cutback in funds to departments and two tuition hikes, prompting students to question its appropriateness. Over the years, pranksters regularly dyed the water gold or added soap to create huge mountains of foam. The fountain was removed just before the Clough Undergraduate Learning Center opened in 2011.

The Transette was a prototype of an automated transit technology installed in the mid-1970s along a quarter-mile route between the student center and one of the parking areas. It was lampooned in the *Technique* for its apparent inability to operate at all. A federal government team walked out of a botched onsite test in 1975, and the project subsequently ran out of money, leaving behind only the derelict cars and a nice new walkway. (Courtesy of the Georgia Tech *Blueprint*.)

Stinger busses, originally just ordinary school busses, have served students for decades, since the campus began to expand beyond reasonable walking distance after World War II. One Stinger-related landmark is the unique bus shelter on Tech Parkway, notorious because its design serves as a freezing cold wind tunnel in winter and provides almost no protection from rain unless it happens to fall straight down.

The student center has been one of the centers of student life since its opening in 1970. It houses a massive cafeteria and food court, a post office, a game room and bowling alley, music listening room, and arts-and-crafts area, and a "hidden in plain sight" de facto faculty lounge. It was, incidentally, also the location of the first campus ATM, "Tilly the All-Time Teller," that even President Pettit had to try out. (Courtesy of the Georgia Tech *Blueprint*.)

Bookstores were at one time one of the locations of central importance for all students. The giant Houston Bookstore was built in the 1970s as an annex to the student center. Packed full of students during the first days of class each term, the bookstore served throughout the year as a place to buy college memorabilia and general interest and faculty-authored books, and of course, sell back used books for a little pocket money when classes were over. It is shown here under construction in 1970.

# *Five*

# CAMPUS ORGANIZATIONS

Georgia Tech's military, cocurricular, honors, Greek, social, and hobby clubs are a diverse and remarkable set of organizations that span the institute's full history. Its military organizations, including the various branches of ROTC, are particularly important, since ROTC service was mandatory for all capable students from the time of World War I to the 1960s. Equally notable are Tech's dozens of Greek organizations, some of which date to the late 19th century. Although just a few of the oldest national fraternities and sororities are mentioned here, there were scores of others, some of which were local, and some of which faded away over time, particularly after the turbulent years of the world wars and the Great Depression. Among the honors societies, the locally-founded ANAK for seniors and Koseme for juniors stand out. Tech also had numerous Greek-letter honors fraternities as well as societies formed around majors, technical areas, or business.

Tech's literary, arts, and music organizations are especially important to campus life and have been remarkably resilient over time, especially given that until very recently, the institute's academic support for the arts and humanities was extremely limited. Besides supporting the long-running and award-winning *Technique* student newspaper and the *Blueprint* yearbook for over a century, there were also several other news publications, humor magazines, and literary journals.

The nature of student organizations has changed over the decades, especially as Tech morphed from an all-male, largely white student body into something much more diverse. Latin American students, for example, had their own club as early as the 1930s. Greek organizations grew—slowly at first—to include a number of traditional sororities, while women followed the pattern of the men in establishing their own technical or major-centered clubs as well.

In the 21st century, it remains to be seen whether internet connectedness and other virtual community building will replace the broad range of "in real life" social organizations. Some of that has already been seen in the decline of co-op program and dormitory-based organizations.

Four seniors, advised by Prof. William H. Emerson, founded ANAK in 1908, and it functioned for many years as the student government and organizer of social events before assuming its present form as an organization for outstanding juniors and seniors. (Graduates and faculty have also been members.) Despite the custom of using capital letters, ANAK is not an acronym for anything; it is apparently named after the biblical Anak, who was father to a race of giants. ANAK members were deeply involved in the creation of several of Tech's institutions, including the *Technique* and the *Blueprint*, as well as student government and the tradition of the freshman "rat cap." Notable members have included Jimmy Carter (honorary), Bobby Dodd, and George P. Burdell.

Dean Skiles created "Take A Prof to Lunch" in 1923 to "establish a connecting link between the faculty and the student body in order that the latter might have a medium through which they could voice their opinions and complaints to the school officials" and manage campus life. That same year, ANAK proposed a new student council, the forerunner to the present Student Government Association. By 1935, the SGA had responsibility for student publications, student discipline, and representation of students at student conventions. It consisted of 24 people representing each class, plus co-op students, the interfraternity council, the president of the YMCA, publications editors, and class presidents. Later iterations would also include representatives from ROTC and the dorms. The graduate senate was created in 1968. From left to right, Rhonda Ragsdale (first female SGA president), Denise Ellis (vice president), and Lisa Johnson (sophomore class president), shown here in 1981–1982, were three of the pioneering female members of the student government.

Tech's first Army ROTC unit, formed in 1918, was ensured of its survival on campus when the faculty voted to make it compulsory for lowerclassmen. In 1926, the Navy expanded its presence, noting the school's excellence in math and science. Preparations for reviving wartime training began quietly in 1937, and at the outbreak of World War II, Tech established or further enhanced several military training programs, including ROTC. The programs were humming along by 1943, when suddenly the largest contingent of student-trainees, the Army Specialized Training Division, was abruptly shipped to Europe in March 1944, markedly draining the campus of students. For some years, the Army ROTC used Rose Bowl Field to practice gunnery with miniature artillery pieces that fired low-charge projectiles at targets that sometimes included traffic on Tenth Street. ROTC service remained compulsory into the 1960s.

The *Blueprint* (called the *Blue Print* until 1956) is Tech's oldest living publication and was first published in 1908. The student newspaper, the *Technique*, first appeared somewhat later in late 1911. The *Technique* is remarkable in part because of the fact that through most of Tech's history, there was no academic literary or journalism program to support it. An earlier, competing publication, the *Yellow Jacket*, appeared about the same time as the *Technique* and evolved into a humor magazine. Its career abruptly ended in 1955 when the faculty voted to shut it down after it published something offensive about Dean George Griffin's secretary. It was replaced by the *Rambler*, which ran from 1956 to at least 1968. Students also published a technical magazine, the *Georgia Tech Engineer*, from 1938 to 1971. The *Technique* staff is shown here.

The North Avenue YMCA served as the focal point of many student activities during Tech's first decades. The Y organized not only the expected Bible studies but also activities such as the *Technique*. By 1970, the organization began to lose its significance on campus due to the opening of the Wenn Student Center and the shift in campus activity from the area around the Administration Building where the Y was located, to the north and west, where new classroom and dorm buildings were being constructed. Today, the YMCA building, separated from campus by a very busy North Avenue (although connected by a pedestrian bridge), overlooks a part of campus that students rarely visit unless a football game is being played. It houses the Alumni Association. (Both, courtesy of the Georgia Tech *Blueprint*.)

While early Tech students gained practical experience in the mandatory shop classes and through arrangements with the Atlanta Water Works (for steam engine operation) and Georgia Railway (for electric generators), the co-operative program did not officially begin until 1912. "Cooperating" employers agreed to pay students 15¢ an hour and guarantee fulltime employment on graduation. Co-op students were in a special academic category and had their own dorms initially before being integrated into the main student body some years later. Internships, which lasted as little as a single quarter, became a second option in the 1960s. The co-op program was not just about work. For many years, co-op students sponsored one of the few summer activities on campus, a Field Day that featured a greased-pig chase as well as a volleyball game between students and notoriously cheating professors.

College drinking clubs are a hoary tradition going back centuries, but puritanical opposition to them in the United States meant that their numbers were subject to periodic binges followed by purges. Little is known about Tech's drinking clubs or even how to distinguish them from related social clubs. Many were probably created to formalize drinking along with related activities such as card-playing, sports, dining, or smoking cigars. Further, the definition of a drinking club is fuzzy, since many organizations, notably fraternities, featured drinking as one of their several main activities. The *Blueprint* at least recorded the existence of what appear to be drinking clubs and sometimes gave clues as to their purpose and activities. There can be no doubt, for example, of the purpose of a group called the Al-Koh-Hol Club, whose members gathered for a photograph that appeared in 1920. But it is also worth mentioning that some historians believe that the "club" photographs for the *Blueprint* were sometimes just pranks, so the truth may never be known. (Courtesy of the Georgia Tech *Blueprint*.)

The first fraternities at Georgia Tech, created between 1888 and 1899, were Alpha Tau Omega, Beta Kappa, Sigma Alpha Epsilon, Sigma Nu, Kappa Alpha, and Kappa Sigma. Beta Theta Pi was the first fraternity to build a house on campus, in 1926. Through much of the 20th century, fraternities served a central social role. Nationally, as membership in Greek organizations waned after the 1950s, fraternities thrived at Tech. Though individual dormitories, honor societies, the co-op clubs, and other organizations also contributed to student life, it was the fraternities that invented and later maintained all of Tech's noted traditions, such as Homecoming festivities, the Ramblin' Wreck Parade, the Ramblin' Raft Race, student publications, and the student government. Fraternities organized events that invited women from local colleges, served copious amounts of alcohol, and generally ensured that a good time was had by all. (Both, courtesy of the Georgia Tech *Blueprint*.)

Sororities began almost as soon as the admission of the first women at Tech. Nearly all of them (five in total) got together in 1954 and formed a chapter of Alpha Xi Delta. Diana Michel, who would become the institute's first female graduate, was president. But the growth in the number of female students was extremely slow, and a second sorority, Alpha Gamma Delta, was not created until almost two decades later, in 1972. Today there are eight traditional sororities, plus three African American sororities, an Asian sorority, a South Asian sorority, a Latina sorority, and a multicultural sorority, the latter reflecting the institute's growing student diversity.

Coach William Alexander created the Yellow Jacket Club in 1930 in an attempt to boost flagging student morale. In subsequent years, the club sponsored and organized events such as the Homecoming Parade and the Freshman Cake Race and, more controversially, the rules imposed on freshmen, particularly rules related to the wearing of so-called rat caps (those rules would be attacked as hazing by the 1960s). During World War II, as membership in many social organizations suffered, the Yellow Jacket Club began to falter, and it was disbanded in 1945. The senior honor society, ANAK, created a replacement called the Ramblin' Reck Club (always spelled without the "w") during the summer of 1945. Today's Ramblin' Reck Club has as one of its major duties the maintenance of the Ramblin' Wreck (always with the "w") Ford automobile. The car was purchased in the early 1960s, and its use was governed by the Student Council until 1967. After that year, Ramblin' Reck members acted as drivers of the car. Today, the Ramblin' Reck Club also organizes the major Homecoming events.

117

Among the many social clubs of the early 20th century were several large Bible study groups, such as the All Saints Bible Class and the Episcopal Club, that met at nearby churches or residences. The YMCA ran the Gene Turner Bible Class and sent a delegation to its annual student conference in the Blue Ridge Mountains. While colleges and universities nationally saw a decline in student interest in religious life after World War II, this was not the case at Georgia Tech. When in the 1960s that national trend reversed, Georgia Tech's already high level of religious participation increased even more, with several of the larger denominational organizations constructing on-campus centers. The Presbyterian Center is shown above. The Wesley Foundation, Newman (Catholic) Club, Baptist Student Union (below), and the Episcopal Church all opened facilities on campus beginning around 1970.

The India Club and the Society of Black Engineers, shown here, are two of the numerous ethnically oriented student clubs formed over the years. Given that Tech was in the segregated South, it is remarkable how many such organizations existed and, sometimes, how early they appeared. One of the first was the Latin American Club. Although little is known about its origins or members, it was featured in the *Blue Print* as early as 1917. Most likely, its members were from Cuba or Puerto Rico, as both countries had active international student exchange programs in the early 20th century. The India Club and various Asian student organizations were post–World War II manifestations of various programs intended to assist in the development of foreign nations. Many members were graduate students or their spouses. Other groups included the AfroAmerican Association, the Lebanon Club, League of United Latin American Citizens, and the Spanish Speaking Organization. (Both, courtesy of the Georgia Tech *Blueprint*.)

Many students, particularly before about 1925, organized themselves into clubs (often short-lived or very informal) based on nostalgia for their home cities or states. Most of the clubs that existed long enough to warrant a photograph in the *Blue Print* or a mention in the *Technique* were based on Georgia cities, reflecting the local origins of most of the student body, but a few represented more remote (usually Southern) states. They included the Americus Boys, the Augusta Club, the Chattanooga Club, the Columbus Club, the Coweta Club, the Elberton Club, the Florida Club, the GeeChee Club of Savannah, the Louisiana State Club, the Macon Club, the Marietta Club, the Mississippians, the North Carolina Club, the Savannah Club, and the Tennessee Club. The Venetian Club, however, was just a social club for night-school students. Members of the Augusta Club are shown above in 1917 and below in 1920. (Both, courtesy of the Georgia Tech *Blueprint*.)

The first Georgia Tech band was informally organized in 1908 by a small group of students. While many student activities were suspended during World War I, the band persisted because of the perceived need for martial music to accompany ROTC military training. Over the years, the military band traveled around the state to perform in parades and other functions. The Glee Club, a singing group, formed in 1906, and its success also led to numerous trips around the state for public and private performances. There were numerous other musical groups formed over the years, memorably the Mandolin Club, made all the more remarkable by the fact that Tech had no academic music program at all until 1963, and students could not even minor in music until the mid-1990s (however, the institute now boasts a graduate degree in music technology). (Both, courtesy of the Georgia Tech *Blueprint*.)

An informal Georgia Tech alumni association had existed since 1896, but a reorganization in 1919 and the hiring of the first paid employee in 1922 marked the beginning of the modern organization. While in the 1890s the alumni association saw itself as a group devoted to ensuring graduates found jobs, by the 1920s, it was also devoted to raising money to support the institute in the face of persistent shortfalls in state support. Membership in the association was paid for with annual dues. Only in 1947 did the association launch the annual Roll Call, where alumni were asked to make donations based on their ability to pay. With the institute's 75th anniversary approaching in 1963, the Georgia Tech Alumni Association launched a major program of self-evaluation, promotion of the institute, and fundraising, the latter of which continued to see growth through the 1960s. Tech's alumni organization began to be nationally recognized for its efforts, and Tech's alumni noted for their high level of giving. The association renovated and occupied the old North Avenue YMCA building (the porch of which is shown here) in 1979.

Tech students over the years have created numerous organizations aimed at participation in various hobbies, notably technology-related. The Motorcycle Club, which gathered for a portrait in 1917, was certainly one of the coolest looking. Other hobby groups over the years included the Amateur Radio Club, the Aikido Club, the Camera Club, the Flying Club, the Parachute Club, the Sports Car Club, and several racing clubs. (Both, courtesy of the Georgia Tech *Blueprint*.)

Georgia Tech students in the early 20th century organized clubs and secret societies similar to fraternities around majors or technical interests. The Civil Crew, for example, was founded in 1909 as an honorary organization for civil engineering upperclassmen. Other such groups included the Textile Society, the Aero Club, the Lint Heads (textiles), the Oil Can Club, the Electrolytes, the Commerce Society, the Agricultural Society, and others. Many of these groups functioned as social clubs, gathering members and guests for special events, such as the Beaux Arts Ball, sponsored by the Architectural Society (Beaux Arts Balls traditionally involve whimsical headgear). (Both, courtesy of the Georgia Tech *Blueprint*.)

DramaTech is Atlanta's oldest continuously operating theater, created by students in 1947. It was the successor to the Marionettes, a group created around 1913 that folded during World War II. The new group had several temporary homes, most notably the former Hemphill Avenue Church of God at the corner of Hemphill Avenue and Ferst Drive, where the seating was improved and actors could use the large stage in the main sanctuary. A number of Tech administrators took an interest in DramaTech over the years, especially Dean James Dull, who helped secure space for the group in the new Ferst Center for the Arts when it was constructed in the early 1990s. (Above, courtesy of the Georgia Tech *Blueprint*; right, courtesy of Troy Halverson.)

Student radio station WREK went on-air in 1968, initially with just 10 watts, but 10 years later, the station could boast 40,000 watts, 24-hour operation, and Dolby. Worth remembering also are various other broadcasting activities on campus, from the long-running amateur Ham station still operated from the electrical engineering building to low-power, unlicensed "pirate" stations, such as the one that broadcast from (and apparently could only be heard inside) Techwood Dorm in the late 1980s and early 1990s. (Courtesy of the Georgia Tech *Blueprint*.)

Founded in 1946, the Yellow Jacket Flying Club allowed members of the Tech community to obtain a pilot's license and fly small aircraft at low cost. Its first aircraft, obtained as war surplus, included two German fighters and a B-29 bomber, although none were flyable. Today the club operates a fleet of four Cessna aircraft at DeKalb-Peachtree Airport in Chamblee, Georgia. Members of the flying club are shown in 1977–1978. (Courtesy of the Georgia Tech *Blueprint*.)

# Bibliography

Bix, Amy Sue. *Girls Coming to Tech!: A History of American Engineering Education for Women*. Cambridge, MA: The MIT Press, 2013.

Brittain, James E. and Robert C. McMath Jr. "Engineers and the New South Creed: The Formation and Early Development of Georgia Tech." *Technology and Culture* 18 (April 1977): 175–201.

Brittain, M.L. *The Story of Georgia Tech*. Chapel Hill, NC: University of North Carolina Press, 1948.

Chastain, Bill. *Jackrabbit: The Story of Clint Castleberry and the Improbable 1942 Georgia Tech Football Season*. Thomaston, ME: Tilbury House Publishers, 2011.

Combes, Richard S. "Technology, Southern Style: Case Studies of High-Tech Firms in Atlanta, 1836–1984." Ph.D. dissertation, Georgia Institute of Technology, 2002.

Drury, Warren E. III. "The Architectural Development of Georgia Tech." Master's thesis, Georgia Institute of Technology, 1984.

Dunn, Lee C. *Cracking the Solid South: The Life of John Fletcher Hanson, Father of Georgia Tech*. Macon, GA: Mercer University Press, 2016.

Griessman, B. Eugene, Sarah Evelyn Jackson, and Annibel Jenkins. *Images and Memories, Georgia Tech: 1885–1985*. Atlanta, GA: Georgia Tech Foundation, 1985.

Griffin, George C. *Griffin—You Are a Great Disappointment to Me: The Tales of Georgia Tech's Dean Emeritus George C. Griffin*. Atlanta, GA: Georgia Tech National Alumni Association, 1971.

*Laying the Foundation of the Technological Research University of the 21st Century, The Clough Years: 1994–2008*. Atlanta, GA: Georgia Tech Foundation, n.d.

McMath, Robert C. Jr., Ronald H. Bayor, James E. Brittain, Lawrence Foster, August W. Giebelhaus, and Germaine M. Reed. *Engineering the New South: Georgia Tech, 1885–1985*. Athens, GA: University of Georgia Press, 1985.

Wallace, Robert B. Jr. *Dress Her in White and Gold: A Biography of Georgia Tech*. Atlanta, GA: Georgia Tech Foundation, 1963.

# Discover Thousands of Local History Books Featuring Millions of Vintage Images

Arcadia Publishing, the leading local history publisher in the United States, is committed to making history accessible and meaningful through publishing books that celebrate and preserve the heritage of America's people and places.

Find more books like this at
**www.arcadiapublishing.com**

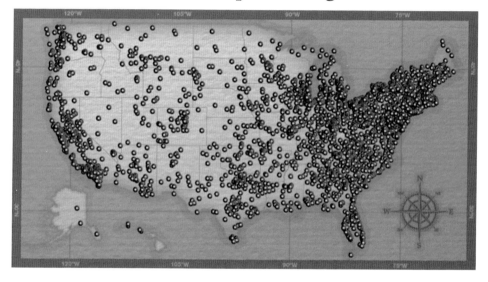

Search for your hometown history, your old stomping grounds, and even your favorite sports team.

Consistent with our mission to preserve history on a local level, this book was printed in South Carolina on American-made paper and manufactured entirely in the United States. Products carrying the accredited Forest Stewardship Council (FSC) label are printed on 100 percent FSC-certified paper.

**MADE IN THE**